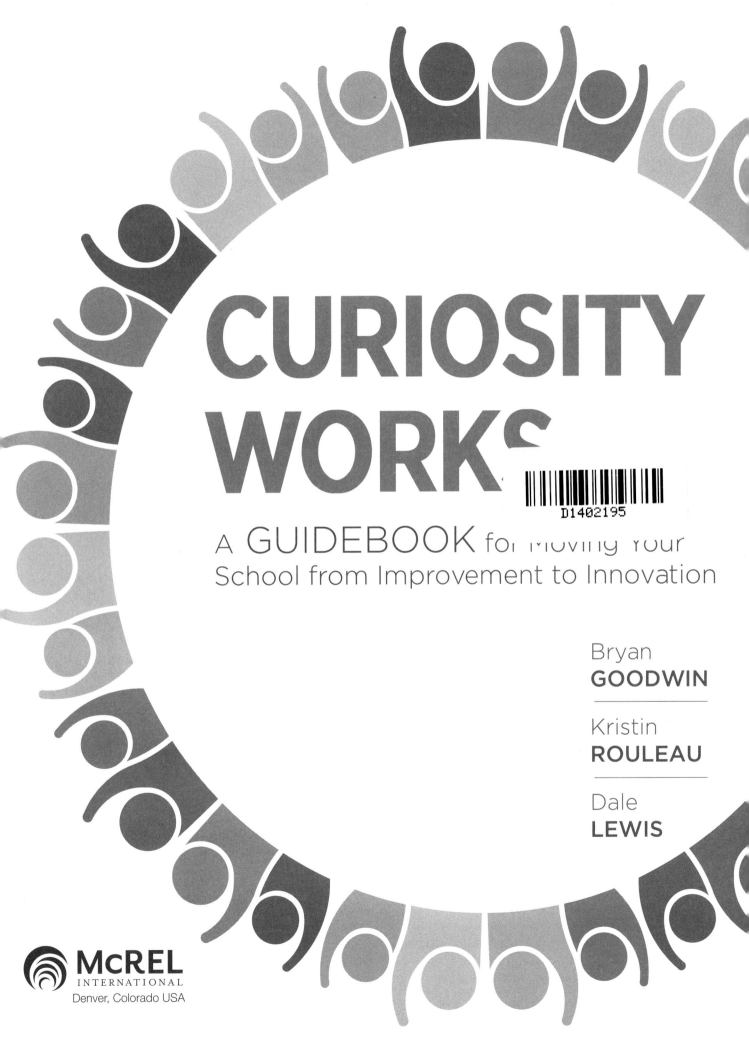

CURIOSITY WORKS

A GUIDEBOOK for Moving Your
School from Improvement to Innovation

Bryan
GOODWIN

Kristin
ROULEAU

Dale
LEWIS

McREL
INTERNATIONAL
Denver, Colorado USA

McREL International

4601 DTC Boulevard, Suite 500

Denver, CO 80237 USA

Phone: 303.337.0990 • Fax: 303.337.3005

Website: www.mcrel.org • Email: info@mcrel.org

About McREL

McREL International helps educators flourish by turning research into solutions that transform teaching, learning, and leading.

McREL is a nonprofit, nonpartisan education research and development organization that since 1966 has turned knowledge about what works in education into practical, effective guidance and training for teachers and education leaders across the U.S. and around the world.

All referenced trademarks are the property of the respective owners. All internet links mentioned in this book are correct as of the initial publication date.

Printed in the United States of America.

To order, visit store.mcrel.org.

ISBN: 978-0-9993549-3-3

Library of Congress Control Number: 2018936168

Goodwin, B., Rouleau, K., & Lewis, D. (2018). *Curiosity works: A guidebook for moving your school from improvement to innovation*. Denver, CO: McREL International.

CURIOSITY WORKS

A GUIDEBOOK for Moving Your
School from Improvement to Innovation

List of Tools

Acknowledgments

The authors gratefully acknowledge Debbie Backus, Sally Chapman, and BJ Worthington for their thoughtful input on the manuscript; Tonia Gibson and Laura Stelling for their innovative work on the school improvement pathways; Ron Miletta, Lisa Maxfield, and Marcellus Lewis for their review and feedback; and the McREL publication team of Roger Fiedler, Judy Counley, Eric Hübler, and Christine H. Schmidt for editing and design.

Introduction

What if all our students came to school eager to learn, self-motivated, and passionate about what they were learning? What if they were, in a word, *curious*?

Wouldn't everything be easier . . . and more joyful?

Student curiosity is a powerful driver of both student success and engagement. It also predicts better relationships, life fulfillment, and job performance (Kashdan & Roberts, 2004; Kashdan & Steger, 2007; Reio & Wiswell, 2000).

So, what would it take for us to create learning environments that unleash student curiosity?

We could begin by unleashing *educators'* professional curiosity, encouraging them to ask questions, build on best practices, and develop *next* practices that create more engaging learning experiences for students. We'd also tap into a yearning most of us feel as professionals: the need to not just survive, but *thrive* in what we do—continuously improving, learning and growing every day, and sharing those learning experiences with other educators in small, learning-focused groups.

That's the assumption at the heart of this guidebook: that the most powerful changes we can make in our schools must come from the *inside out,* from the natural curiosity and intrinsic motivation that everyone shares to experience the joy of learning, discovery, and improvement.

If you're seeking a simple fix for your school or a "silver bullet" to transform your school overnight, you won't find it here (or anywhere for that matter).

What you'll find here, instead, is a way to move *your* school forward, whether it's struggling, cruising, or excelling. Yes, this guidebook will help you find some "quick wins" for achieving short-term gains, but more important, it will help you chart a course to *innovation*: putting the right elements in place to design and build a school where teachers operate as true professionals, developing *precision without prescription*—improving practices not with scripted, one-size-fits-all programs, but rather by supporting teachers in becoming experts who can diagnose and solve student learning challenges and create personalized learning environments that challenge students and allow curiosity to flourish.

The Approach

Over the past 20 years, school improvement and reform efforts have increasingly been driven by top-down, high-stakes accountability systems that are designed to motivate performance by rewarding and penalizing schools based largely on students' performance on standardized achievement tests.

In places, this approach has lifted the overall achievement of students and narrowed the gaps in performance among various student sub-groups (Reardon, Robinson-Cimpian, & Weathers, 2014) and appears to have improved graduation rates (Kamenetz & Turner, 2016). Yet despite some positive outcomes, in state after state and district after district, top-down approaches to improving schools and districts have experienced a plateau effect, producing diminishing returns (Goodwin, Cameron, & Hein, 2015).

What is needed now, at least in schools experiencing these plateaus, is a paradigm shift in our thinking and approach to improvement, one that pivots toward expertise and innovation and emphasizes internally driven accountability and curiosity.

We've seen the power of taking inside-out approaches to improvement while working with schools and school systems from around the nation and the world—including small rural schools in South Dakota, mid-sized districts in Nebraska and Tennessee, rapidly improving systems in the Pacific, and a large urban system in Australia that faced similar challenges, societal changes, and student needs as those in the United States. In the large, diverse Northern Metropolitan Region of Melbourne, with 70,000-plus students, McREL's Curiosity Works™ approach to school improvement and innovation has been generating gains in student learning, engagement, and teacher practice by stimulating curiosity and supporting collaborative inquiry.

This guidebook describes how you, too, can promote curiosity and a culture of collaboration for teaching, learning, and leading to re-energize your school.

The Knowledge Base

The Curiosity Works approach is built on a solid foundation of research and best practice, including McREL's research over the past two decades on effective school systems, schools, leadership, and instruction, as reported in such books as:

- *School Leadership That Works: From Research to Results* (2001)

- *District Leadership That Works: Striking the Right Balance* (2009)

- *Simply Better: Doing What Matters Most to Change the Odds for Student Success* (2011)

- *Classroom Instruction That Works: Research-Based Strategies for Increasing Student Achievement*, 2nd ed. (2012)

- *The 12 Touchstones of Good Teaching: A Checklist for Staying Focused Every Day* (2013)

- *Balanced Leadership for Powerful Learning: Tools for Achieving Success in Your School* (2015)

On a more practical level, it's also built on what we have learned from our work nationally and internationally to engage school communities in a rigorous process of improvement and innovation at the classroom, leadership, and system levels. In Melbourne, for example, focusing on curiosity and inside-out approaches to change raised both the floor and the ceiling for students in a large system with a history of chronic low performance (Hopkins, 2011). And in the 35,000-student Clarksville-Montgomery County School System, the "plain vanilla" reform of focusing on creating more consistency in teaching and student learning experiences resulted in the highest student growth rate of any district in Tennessee.

Students, as might be expected, were the first to notice changes in the practice of their teachers in Melbourne. Both during and following the initial four years of implementation of a Curiosity Works approach, annual student surveys regarding perceptions of teacher effectiveness showed that students in every grade level measured (grades 5–12) perceived their teachers' effectiveness to be increasing, rating their teachers at or better than the average for teachers across the state of Victoria.

At the heart of this book is what we believe to be a profound insight about school improvement and change gleaned from examining what happens when school systems worldwide transform, as well as how "high-reliability" organizations (HRO) in such fields as aviation and wildland fire-fighting strive to deliver perfect performance every day because lives depend on it. It's this: While local context often varies from school to school, the pathways to improvement—the things schools must do to move from low-performing to high-performing to innovative—look remarkably similar, following predictable stages of improvement that require different approaches to leadership and professional learning.

> **What's an *HRO*?**
>
> A high-reliability organization (HRO) has routine procedures in place that reduce the chances of catastrophes, even in complex, high-risk businesses where accidents can be expected. Some common HRO principles that schools can use include monitoring and assessing everyday processes and outcomes; anticipating and remediating potential complications before they happen; training staff often on routines and best practices; and encouraging a resilient mindset when facing obstacles and change.

Changing from the Inside Out

This guidebook is not a one-size-fits-all approach to improvement, but a practical, research-based road map to guide you on your journey. We have designed it to help school leadership teams make the pivot from top-down, *outside-in* improvement to school-owned (and even teacher-owned), *inside-out* innovation that's required as school teams move toward greater professional expertise and innovation.

We cannot make external accountability pressures go away—nor should we, as they often provide an initial spark to encourage better practice. But we can change how we *respond* to those pressures as school leaders and leadership teams. This guidebook is designed to help school leadership teams engage everyone in their schools in a different approach to improvement and innovation—one that taps into people's intrinsic motivation, including their natural curiosity to learn and innate desire to achieve what the 20th-century American psychologist Abraham Maslow (1943) described as *self-actualization*. In our own research and experience, we've found this to be a more powerful, productive, and joyful approach to change in schools—one that can address near-term improvement needs (i.e., "quick wins") while at the same time creating the structures, dispositions, and skills needed to engage in game-changing, rapid-cycle innovation. The result? Schools where students are inspired by what may be the most powerful driver of learning: *curiosity*.

Briefly, an inside-out approach reflects these guiding principles:

1. **Create shared moral purpose.** Instead of using a "because-I-said-so" rationale, we start with a deep conversation and reflection among stakeholders in a school about *why*, getting everyone on the same page and committing to shared purpose for education.

2. **Start with motivation, engagement, and curiosity**. Rather than create a system that revolves around test scores and grades, we start with student *and teacher* motivation and engagement, tapping into the power of curiosity.

3. **Build on bright spots**. Because the best answers often lie within "positive deviants" or "bright spots" in our current practices, we seek out these bright spots in classrooms and find ways to leverage what's already working more broadly and consistently.

4. **Lead with questions**. Real solutions come from better insights, which means school leaders and teachers must ask powerful questions about teaching and learning to help everyone engage in root cause analysis and reflective learning.

5. **Support change with peer coaching**. To truly change practice, we must engage in peer coaching. This means teachers working together in small teams to hone best practices identified from bright spots in the system. Or they may create their own bright spots through collaborative study and practice.

6. **Adopt and *adapt* in rapid cycles**. Because *threat* conditions are counterproductive, we instead need to create conditions that *challenge* and encourage people to "fail forward" in rapid improvement cycles that drive greater precision of teaching practice.

7. **Reframe the goal and fail forward**. What we measure is what gets done, so we must use more robust measures for student learning and success as we encourage people to "fail fast" and "fail forward"—using data to learn what's working and what's not to guide rapid-cycle improvement and innovation.

What's a *rapid improvement cycle*?

An organization using a rapid improvement cycle identifies, implements, and measures changes to a process or system over the course of just a few days, weeks, or months, rather than waiting for an entire semester or school year to pass. Often, rapid improvement cycle efforts follow a Plan-Do-Study-Act format.

What's *failing forward*?

Failing forward is a mindset of viewing struggles and failures not as summative events, but as an expected, natural part of the learning process. When students (and educators themselves) view failure as a formative moment, or an opportunity, they can then use the "failed" outcome to reflect on what happened, explore the lessons learned, and plan new pathways forward. A fail-forward attitude strengthens resiliency and perseverance when tackling challenges, and creates an environment in which students are comfortable taking academic risks and using feedback.

Creating a Research and Innovation Team (RIT)

We've written this guidebook for school leadership (or instructional leadership) teams—something we'll refer to throughout as a *Research and Innovation Team* (RIT). The RIT should play a central role in your school's inside-out improvement and innovation journey. It will serve as the "research and development" group responsible for monitoring and supporting the day-to-day improvement and innovation work in your school.

The RIT should be an instrumental force in guiding every aspect of your journey: determining readiness, assessing and facilitating the conditions for change, establishing a focus, engaging in collaborative inquiry, and monitoring and supporting the development of a culture of inquiry.

The Importance of Shared Leadership

A key assumption through this guidebook is that leadership is most effective when it's *shared*.

A growing body of research indicates that developing shared leadership leads to increased positive outcomes for individuals and teams. Although scholars first began writing about the concept of shared leadership in the 1950s, few empirical studies on the topic emerged in the literature until recently. These studies (Carson, Tesluck, & Marrone, 2007; Nicolaides et al., 2014; Pearce & Conger, 2003; Zhang, Waldman, & Wang, 2012) demonstrate positive relationships between shared leadership and increased team efficacy, effort, collaboration and coordination, innovative problem solving, satisfaction, citizenship behavior, and performance.

Considerations for the Research and Innovation Team

When building a school's RIT, it's important to bring together individuals who are willing to invest time and energy in improving the school—whether it's already a high-performing organization, or one in need of some significant changes. RITs often meet monthly at a minimum (we know of schools where they meet weekly) with a focus on examining data, current practices, and research about best practices, and planning for implementation and monitoring of strategies to support teaching and learning. Because school improvement is a continuous process, it's a good idea to have members serve for more than a year, and for membership to rotate so there are always experienced voices and new voices at the table.

In bringing the team together, it's also important to consider the staff perspectives represented. Select membership across grade levels, subjects, specialty areas, teacher experience, tenure in your school, etc. In addition, it's important to be sure your team brings an assets-oriented approach; the work of school improvement requires a belief that the students in your school can and will learn at high levels. This is important because ultimately, your RIT will be the "keepers of the flame" of your school's moral purpose, helping everyone connect what you're doing back to a deeper sense of purpose.

Four Key Reflection Questions for RIT Members:

- As RIT members, how do you maintain focus on your school as a whole, taking a systems perspective rather than focusing solely on your area of daily responsibility?

- When competing demands emerge, and energy for improvement and innovation subsides, how do you help staff stay focused on improving?

- What systems does the RIT have in place for reviewing progress toward goals?

- What information does the RIT collect about how individuals and teams are experiencing and managing change? How is this information collected?

Figure 1. Implementation phases for an inquiry-driven culture of continuous improvement

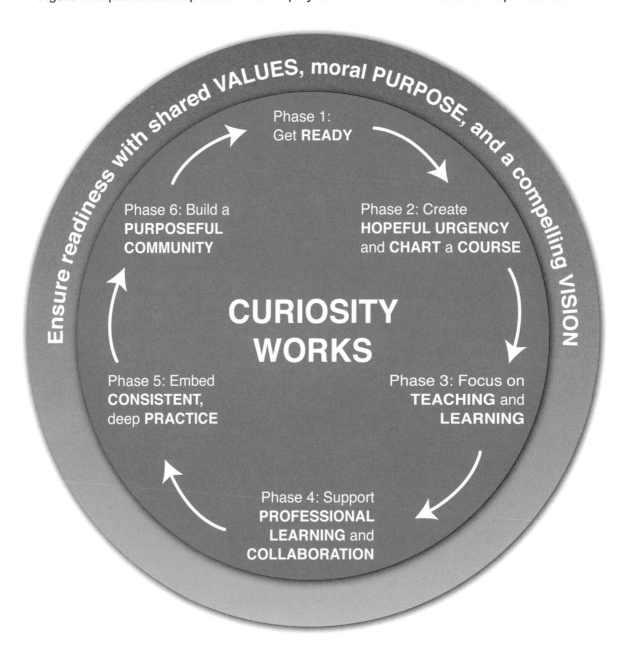

Using this Guidebook

This guidebook translates the principles of inside-out change—as well as our extensive research on leadership development and school improvement—into a straightforward, six-phase process you can follow to support ongoing, inside-out innovation and an inquiry-driven culture in your school (see Figure 1 on page 6).

We'll also help you build readiness by creating a purposeful community in your school, one guided by shared moral purpose and values.

We've arranged this guidebook to help you and your RIT guide your school through each phase of this journey, providing you with insights and tools to support you in this work.

To illustrate the phases of this journey, we've aggregated the experiences of real schools we've worked with into a semi-fictional narrative of one school's journey to innovation.

For the sake of simplicity, we've arranged the phases of development as a sequence, but you'll likely find that, in practice, the process of innovation is "messier" and less linear than a step-by-step process; you may find the need to revisit earlier stages or jump ahead to subsequent phases. That's OK. Indeed, innovative schools consistently report that while they often "beg, borrow, and steal" from others, in the end, they make the process their own, adapting what others have done to their own needs (Goodwin, 2017).

Fair warning: While targeting key leverage points will help you achieve "quick wins," the journey we outline in this guidebook is not a quick *fix*. We do not offer simple, one-size-fits-all tips and tricks for "fixing" your school in a matter of weeks, but rather, a more comprehensive, thoughtful approach to helping you create a long-term, inspiring vision for your school and chart a course for moving closer to that vision every day.

Don't expect that you and your school team will be able to progress through all six phases and 17 tools in a matter of days or a few weeks. It could take several months or more to work your way through the phases of development, and even then you won't be "done." You'll probably revisit sections of this guidebook from time to time during a continuous cycle of improvement and innovation. But we promise: The outcomes of the journey will be worth the investment. Your students will benefit from deeper, more engaging learning and your teachers will soon experience the rewards of working together to create more powerful and joyful learning in their classrooms.

So, are you ready to begin? Or maybe a little concerned about how this is going to work?

Don't worry, we're here to guide you along the way. Let's ease into our effort with the first installment in the story of the journey of our school, Stillbrook K–8 School.

Phase 1: Get Ready

What's our guiding purpose and how do we work together?

Stuck in a Rut

It was late May, and the leadership team at Stillbrook K–8 School felt exhausted and defeated. For three years, their achievement data had flatlined and even declined in some areas—a frustrating outcome after three prior years of sustained progress during which the school had been lauded by state and district officials, and by glowing headlines in the local newspaper.

Now things felt bleak, even though everyone was working harder than before, especially members of the school's leadership team, who jocularly tried to shoo one another out of the building long after the school doors had closed. Recently, Oscar Blanco, the assistant principal, found the name badge of his principal, Janice Brown, in the mail room while working late one night and went to put it in her office. He startled a bit when he found her sitting at her desk. As he handed the name badge to her, he joked, "You might need to start wearing this at home if you don't start spending less time here and more time there."

"You, too," she replied. "And you've got young kids at home. You should go home to them."

At their next leadership meeting—the last one of the year, in early June—Janice looked at the faces of her leadership team as they chatted quietly before the meeting. They all looked tired. Student test results weren't back yet—it would be a few more months before they saw them—but judging by the district interim assessments, it was likely they'd see similarly flat results, if not a bit worse, despite a year-long focus on close reading and argumentation in mathematics.

"So, I have a question for everyone. Why are you doing this?" she asked, immediately getting the team's attention. "*Education*, I mean. Why did you get into this profession?"

After a few moments, Tom Green, the outgoing and outdoorsy science teacher who also served as the middle school's instructional coach, answered first. "I guess I'm kind of a nerd who comes from a long line of educators. I love seeing light bulbs go on for kids when they finally grasp a concept. You know, that *aha moment*. It's priceless. I think that's what keeps me coming back year after year."

Belinda Gold, a veteran 4th-grade teacher and part-time coach for the elementary grade teachers, was known for being a "kooky serious" teacher, doing things like taking her students out to the school yard for a ritual burial of over-used words. "The fat paycheck, of course," she said to chuckles from the group. "Seriously, though, it's along the lines of what Tom said: I love young minds and the questions they ask. There's never a dull moment in teaching—if you do it right."

As usual, Oscar, quiet and introspective, went last. "I grew up a poor kid, so my parents ingrained in me the value of education as a ticket to a better life. That's why I got into education—to improve kids' life chances."

"Wow, can I have Oscar's answer?" Belinda said with a smile. "So, how about you, Janice?

Why are you doing this—killing yourself to be a principal?"

Janice Brown was serious to the core; there was nothing kooky about her. When she arrived at the school seven years earlier, she had established order and routines, like regular visits to classrooms and data team meetings. She carved funds out of the school budget to let Tom and Belinda serve as part-time instructional coaches. And she made teaching and learning THE discussion topic during staff meetings, while quietly counseling a few teachers out of the school and replacing them with better ones. For a few years, those changes worked. Teaching practices improved and test scores climbed. She was credited for turning around the school and seen as a rising star in the district. Then, inexplicably, Stillbrook K–8 School hit a plateau. Test scores went flat. Janice kept pressing harder, but to no avail.

In response to Belinda's question, she took off her glasses and rubbed her eyes. "To tell you the truth, I didn't like school much when I was a kid. We were a military family and moved around a lot, usually living off-base. So, I was in and out of a lot of schools. Kids can be cruel, especially to the new kid. And I was *always* the new kid. My self-esteem was pretty much in the toilet."

Everyone in the room was surprised, given the air of self-confidence Janice projected.

"In 10th grade, I had an amazing English teacher who took a shine to me. One day when I was walking out of class, she stopped me and said, 'You're going to be a leader someday.' I was floored. I'd never thought of myself that way. But it stuck with me. I studied business in college, thinking maybe I'd lead a company. But I kept coming back to how that one teacher had changed my life. I really don't remember what she taught me, but I remember how she made me *feel*. So, as a senior in college, I changed majors to education, hoping to change kids' lives the same way."

"Thanks for sharing that," Belinda said. "I never knew that about you. So, what made you ask about us?"

Janice looked around the room. "To confirm what I suspected: that we're all *driven* to do this work and deeply passionate about what we're doing. Which is why I don't understand something."

"What's that?" Belinda asked.

"Why are we all feeling this way . . . so *miserable?*"

The others were taken aback by the word *miserable* and protested a bit. Janice asked them how many times per week they experienced joy while at work. The room fell silent.

"That's what I thought. Look, maybe I've done that. I know I can be tough on you at times. But can you do me a favor? First, please come back here in August. Second, let's spend the summer catching up on our professional reading and imagining what kind of school we want to be and how to get there. What would it take to create a place that teachers and students love coming to? To be honest, I know we need to do *something* differently; we still have too many kids who aren't doing well. But frankly, and it's hard to admit this, I'm out of ideas for what to do. I need your help."

As everyone filed out of the room, Oscar turned to Janice. "You're a good leader, Dr. Brown. The best I've ever had. Take a look at what you just did there: You connected us all back to what's important to us. That's *leadership*. So, don't worry. We'll figure this out together."

"Thanks, Oscar," Janice replied. "And maybe this summer, you can do me a favor."

"What's that?"

"When you have a spare moment, maybe you can think about what *that*"—she pointed at the school's mission statement poster on the wall—"should say."

Oscar shot a glance at the poster with the current mission statement:

Stillbrook K–8 School seeks to create a challenging learning environment with high expectations for all students that fosters academic excellence through developmentally appropriate instruction that allows for individual differences and learning styles. Stillbrook promotes a safe, orderly, caring, and supportive environment that fosters each student's self-esteem through positive relationships with students and staff. We strive to actively engage our parents, teachers, and community members in our students' learning.

"I've read that mission statement a hundred times or more, but as I look at it again, I'm not sure what it really says—and I was on the committee that wrote it," she confessed. "There's nothing particularly *wrong* with it, but there's nothing particularly *inspiring* about it either."

"Oh, is that what it's supposed to do? Inspire us?" Oscar asked with a smile.

"Ideally, yes," she replied. "But for now, it would be *ideal* if you'd go home to your family." ■

Committing to Shared Values

In our research on high-performing schools, McREL has found that school organizational culture is the "secret sauce" of school performance—it's what makes change possible for some schools and impossible for others (Goodwin, 2011). Basically, every organization has a set of rules—often unspoken—by which it operates.

High-performing schools, for example, embrace collegiality, open dialogue, and honest, reflective examination of their data. In this spirit of "kaizen," the Japanese business philosophy of continuous improvement, every system defect that is identified is viewed as a treasure pointing toward opportunities to improve practice.

Dysfunctional, low-performing schools, on the other hand, tend to view data more as a *window* (showing them what others are doing wrong or must do) than as a *mirror* (showing what they must do *themselves* to get better).

We'll return to this idea about data, but our point here is that all schools have written and unwritten rules that guide their behaviors. Like mission statements, values can be bland pronouncements that fail to specify what truly distinguishes a school's culture. They can be wishful thinking included in a wall poster that doesn't reflect how people *really* behave. Moreover, a school's *real* values may remain tacit or unspoken, yet plainly evident in the choices people make in a school—for example, when more desirable teaching assignments, like honors classes or teacher leadership positions, are doled out on the basis of seniority instead of merit. Such behaviors suggest that the school leaders place adults' desires above students' needs—hardly a value any school would state explicitly in a poster hanging on the wall.

As your school engages in the work of improvement and innovation, it's important to clarify the core values that drive your work. Patrick Lencioni (2002), a CEO, author, and consultant in leadership and management, offers a helpful way to think about four types of values:

- *Core* values—two or three traits that truly define an organization.

    We hold ourselves and each other to high standards for teaching and learning.

    We believe all of our students can go to college.

- *Aspirational* values—traits that don't yet define the organization but everyone agrees are necessary, such as innovation or collegiality.

    We adopt and adapt in rapid cycles in order to provide students with the instruction they need, when they need it.

    We are innovative in our curriculum development and delivery.

- *Accidental* values—unwritten (and often counterproductive) rules that reflect how people act or treat one another.

    We believe more experienced teachers have the best ideas (a counterproductive accidental value).

    We actively work to make sure everyone has a voice in decision making (a productive accidental value).

- *Permission-to-play* values—behaviors that are important but don't necessarily define an organization, such as treating others with dignity and respect.

    We only hire teachers who believe ALL kids can learn. There is no place in our school for a teacher who thinks some kids can't learn.

    We view differences as opportunities for everyone to learn, not as something that needs to be changed.

An organization's list of values ought to answer these critical questions:

- How do we behave, especially when no one is looking?

- What behaviors have we cultivated over time that distinguish us from other schools?

- What do we value so much we're willing to make sacrifices for it?

This last question is an important one, because ultimately, your organizational values should attract the right people and repel the wrong ones. For example, if you include "collegiality" and "lifelong learning" in your list of values, you should be willing to tell people who don't reflect those values they don't fit with your culture and need to change their behavior or seek a position elsewhere.

The tool on the following page will help you review your current values and/or identify new ones.

Tool #1: Identifying shared values

This tool will help you articulate your school's core values by focusing on the traits you recognize in teachers and school staff you consider to be exceptional—those people who consistently perform at a high level and maintain a positive attitude, both when things are going smoothly *and* when there are bumps in the road.

Ask each member of your team to complete steps 1 and 2 individually.

1. Using the shared values diagram in Figure 2, identify your school's "stars" in terms of attitude and performance (the upper-right box).

Figure 2. Shared values diagram

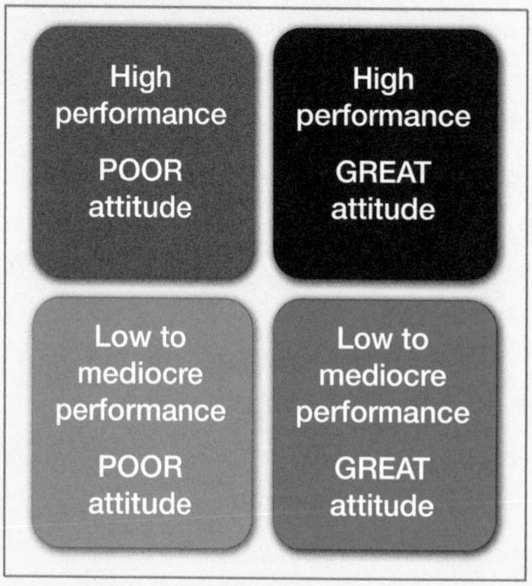

High performance POOR attitude	High performance GREAT attitude
Low to mediocre performance POOR attitude	Low to mediocre performance GREAT attitude

2. List the behaviors and dispositions that make these people special.

_____

_____

_____

_____

_____

3. Now, as a group, each person shares one example of someone who exemplifies "high performance, great attitude," including the behaviors and dispositions they identified as describing their "star." Make a list of these behaviors and attitudes on a chart or board where everyone can see it. When all the stars and attributes have been shared, move on to the discussion in the following steps.

4. What do these behaviors and dispositions say about what these "stars" value? For example, a teacher characterized as "always goes above and beyond for students" may exemplify the core value, "We believe every student can learn more and our job is to be creative in helping them learn as much as possible."

5. Review your list to see if any can be consolidated into a single value.

6. Identify which behaviors/dispositions are *core* vs. *aspirational* vs. *accidental* vs. *permission-to-play* values (refer to the definitions on page 11).

7. Next, we're going to focus on just the core and aspirational values. Ask team members to reflect on the discussion and select 3–7 core and/or aspirational values. Have each person place a dot or a checkmark next to their selected values on the list.

8. Reflect on the selections made by team members. Circle any values that have consensus for being on the final list. Allow each team member the opportunity to make a case for including additional values, and work to agree on your list of 3–7 core and/or aspirational values.

9. Review your list with these questions in mind:

   • *Are we more committed to these values than most other schools?*

   • *Which of these values feel most natural to us and can be done without reminders?*

   • *Are we willing to make sacrifices for these values, such as engaging in difficult personnel conversations, saying no to parents, turning down funding that comes with strings attached, and holding one another accountable for our actions?*

   • *How different would our school look if our behaviors always reflected these values?*

10. Once you've arrived at your final list, use a memorable or meaningful word or phrase to describe each. Avoid tired phrases or expressions. "Commit to excellence" might instead be "Going to 11." You may wish to break into pairs or triads to brainstorm some possible ideas for this step, assigning each small group one or more values to work on.

11. After a few minutes of small group work, bring the group back together to share the creative ideas that were generated. Agree on the final phrases you'll add to your list.

On pages 98–117, you'll find a document we're calling a ToolTracker. We encourage you to use it as you work through the various tools you'll encounter in this guidebook. The ToolTracker is a single place where you can collect the big ideas from the tools, resulting in a comprehensive collection of artifacts you can use as you plan for improvement. As you work through this guidebook, turn to the ToolTracker each time you see the paper-pencil icon, to record data from the tools you've recently worked through.

Turn to page 98 and record your school's aspirational or core values in the ToolTracker, including the memorable words or phrases you generated.

Committing to Moral Purpose

"People don't buy what you do, they buy why you do it," observes Simon Sinek (2011) in his book, *Start with Why*. Case in point: Apple Inc.'s customers gladly pay a hefty premium for products that serve the same function as less expensive products. Moreover, many people willingly buy a variety of products—TVs, music players, and phones—from Apple, a *computer* company, yet people have shown they're far less willing to buy those things from other computer companies, like Dell or HP. What's different about Apple? Through their advertising, marketing, and product design, they make clear that they're all about *upending the status quo*. That's their *why*. Every new product attempts to do something radically different than what's been done before.

In contrast, most companies and leaders start from the outside-in, communicating *what*, not *why*, according to Sinek. Apple's competitors, in essence, ask customers, "Hey, do you want to buy a computer from us?" This often evokes a *meh* response. Apple asks, "Hey, do you want to challenge the status quo with us?" The reason this message is so powerful is that it's an *inside-out* approach—one that starts with what's deep inside the psyches of Apple's customers.

We might say the same thing of school change efforts: What people are likely to find more compelling is not the *what* (e.g., ensuring everyone follows the curriculum guides), but the *why* (e.g., providing every student with a pathway to a fulfilling life). Digging deeper into this "why" by asking ourselves, "Why should we provide every student with a pathway to a fulfilling life?" can spur us to reflect more deeply on the values we share as educators and help us to arrive at the core purpose that keeps us returning day after day. This moral purpose, as Fullan (2001) has called it, is an essential component in driving the change necessary to yield the student learning outcomes we desire and students deserve (Bezzina, 2007).

Fullan describes England's National Literacy and Numeracy Strategy implemented in the late 1990s as having generated strong *external* commitment among educators, resulting in improved literacy and numeracy outcomes for all students. Although the strategy was effective in raising student achievement and reflects our own experiences with recent education reform in the U.S., Fullan expressed concern that the pursuit of higher achievement scores also has negative consequences, namely the narrowing of curriculum, a focus on test-taking skills, and more burnout among educators as they pursue increasingly higher achievement targets. To go deeper, Fullan says, strategies to foster *internal* commitment are needed, ones that leverage shared a moral purpose.

Basically, when schools succeed it's for big, important reasons, like serving others, fulfilling a purpose, or upending some set of "rules" to make the world a better place. Indeed, when McREL synthesized decades of research on effective school leadership, we found that several behaviors and dispositions (called leadership responsibilities) clustered into helping school communities gel around a common purpose. Thus, we advise leaders to build "purposeful" communities, starting with articulating shared outcomes that matter to everyone, outcomes that typically relate to making the world a better place. Simply stated, at the heart of every effective school is a clear sense of *moral purpose*.

The following tool will help you and your leadership team—and ultimately your entire school—come together to define your shared moral purpose.

Tool #2: Finding shared moral purpose

As a team, take a moment to revisit the core and aspirational values you identified in Tool #1. Your sense of moral purpose should be firmly rooted in your shared commitment to these values. Before moving forward, ensure (once again) that your team is in consensus regarding the values you identified. Keep your shared values close at hand. They will serve as touchpoints as you discuss your moral purpose.

For this action tool, you will need paper, pens/pencils, a whiteboard or chart paper, and the members of your RIT.

Sit with your team members around a conference table or other shared workspace. Begin by responding with one sentence to each of the following questions. Use one piece of paper for each question.

- Why did *you* become an educator?

- What do *we* hope for each of our students?

When all team members have completed their responses, and beginning with the first question, ask each member to pass their paper to the person on their left. Then, team members read the statement they have received, underlining words or phrases that resonate with them. Next, pass papers once more to the left and each team member completes the reading/underlining steps once again. Words or phrases that are already underlined may be underlined a second time if they are significant to the second reader. Continue this process, passing notes to the left until each is returned to its original author. Phrases underlined multiple times reflect importance to the group.

Next, write each of the underlined words or phrases on the whiteboard or chart paper for all team members to see. Using these words and phrases, the team collaborates to craft a single statement that reflects a shared response to the question, "Why did *you* become an educator?"

Now, repeat the same process for the second question, "What do *we* hope for each of our students?"

Once your team has drafted shared responses to both questions, work together to create one shared statement of moral purpose that connects everyone's reasons for becoming educators to your shared hopes and dreams for your students. Use the sentence stem: At our school, we believe _____.

This process can be replicated with your faculty, possibly in grade- or department-level teams, or as small groups in a faculty meeting, combining the common ideas into a shared moral purpose reflecting input of all staff.

It's OK if the statement of shared moral purpose is somewhat unrefined. It's meant to speak to the *heart*, not the *head*. At some later date, you may wish to polish the statement into something to put on a poster or your school's website, but for now, the main point is to dare to dream, be idealistic, and speak from the heart.

Turn to page 99 and use the ToolTracker to record your team's Statement of Moral Purpose. Notice how it reflects the core values you've already listed.

Embracing the "Vision Thing"

Some school leaders may feel that it's a waste of time to spend too much energy on something as seemingly ethereal as a vision. And in some regards, they're right: A vision need not be excessively polished or wordsmithed. Rather, it ought to capture, in simple and concise terms, your school's aspirations for the future. In that regard, your RIT will likely experience diminished returns if it gets too hung up on trying to craft the exact right vision statement or make it too clever. A vision statement should not be a literary exercise, but something that every member of your RIT (and hopefully school community) can answer, off the cuff, in more or less the same terms, when someone asks (in the school parking lot, at a school board meeting, or a community event) where your school is going.

> **What's the difference between a mission and a vision?**
>
> No one knows for sure. OK, we're kidding . . . but only slightly. Mission and vision statements are often conflated—even on Fortune 500 company websites. With the caveat that their definitions fall more in the realm of philosophy than empirical research, we offer this distinction: A mission statement captures your sense of purpose and is unlikely to change over time, whereas a vision statement attempts to paint a picture of an ideal future and should change over time (unless you seek monotony). Basically, your mission defines why you exist and your vision paints a picture of where you're going.

And yes, it's likely that if you're in a district, your school district may also have a vision, so your school's vision ought to be compatible with that larger vision. Nonetheless, people *in* your school should understand where *your* school is going over the next few years. Indeed, in our own research we've found that one of the reasons people resist change is they're not clear about, or inspired by, the big picture of what they're being asked to do. Thus, if principals and their school leadership teams ignore the "vision thing," they're likely to encounter resistance to change and experience tough sledding. Moreover, studies of effective school turnaround efforts found that the key attribute of these schools is that their leaders *inspired* people to go the extra mile by painting a clear picture of success while sending a strong, positive message that change is not only necessary, but achievable (Brinson, Kowal, & Hassell, 2008).

The next phases of your journey will help you to put some finer detail around your vision, by helping you identify, in more precise terms, what steps you've already taken, and what steps remain to be taken, to achieve your vision for success.

Keeping It Simple

Ultimately, the best visions are often simple statements that capture big ideas—ideas that seem just a bit beyond your reach, yet flow naturally from your moral purpose or mission statement. Here are a few examples from businesses and nonprofit organizations:

Southwest Airlines

- Mission: *Connect people to what's important in their lives through friendly, reliable, low-cost air travel.*

- Vision: *To become the world's most loved, most flown, and most profitable airline.*

Zappos.com

- Mission: *To provide the best customer service possible (delivering the WOW).*

- Vision: *One day, 30% of all retail transactions in the U.S. will be online. People will buy from the company with the best service and the best selection. Zappos.com will be that online store.*

Make-a-Wish Foundation

- Mission: *Grant the wishes of children with life-threatening medical conditions to enrich the human experience with hope, strength and joy.*

- Vision: *Making every eligible child's wish come true.*

Save the Children

- Mission: *To inspire breakthroughs in the way the world treats children and to achieve immediate and lasting change in their lives.*

- Vision: *A world in which every child attains the right to survival, protection, development and participation.*

When creating and sharing visions for school improvement and innovation, keep this rule in mind: the simpler, the better. Ideally, a single compelling idea will drive your vision, which can be captured in a simple phrase that people can grasp and internalize.

Our next tool can help you put a "title" on your narrative—a simple phrase that everyone on your RIT can repeat over and over. Once you hear teachers and other stakeholders repeating the phrase and describing what it means, you'll know you've found a good way to frame your vision.

Tool #3: Framing your vision

At times, a framing device can help broadcast your message to a wider audience. By framing your vision a bit differently, you may find it resonates with or is more readily understood by your entire school community.

Framing devices aren't meant to replace your core message, but to provide a shorthand way of talking about it. Use this tool to brainstorm some possible framing devices that can help you explain your vision in just a few words. You might have each member of your team work independently on these, have partners team up, or engage in some creative idea generation as a whole team.

Framing device	Description	Example	Apply this device to your narrative
Metaphor	An analogous approach that can be applied to yours.	"We'll take a 'Silicon Valley' approach to rapid-cycle innovation."	
Catch phrase	A brief slogan that captures your intended outcome.	"2 in 1" (2 years of student learning for every year in school).	
Exemplar	A model or vicarious experience to emulate.	"Become the Harlem Children's Zone of our district."	
Depiction	A memorable string of modifiers that reflects your aspirations.	"Students who are capable, caring, and curious."	
Visual image	A captivating picture that helps people see what's possible.	"Helping every student—even those who dislike school—love learning."	

On page 100, in the ToolTracker, record the one or two framing statements that best describe your vision. Remember, this is meant as a quick title that everyone can refer to and that the RIT can use to consistently and continuously remind the entire school community of where your school is headed.

From Readiness to Urgency

In this chapter, you've spent time examining and articulating your school's core values and purpose, and you've put words to your vision—where you want to see your school in a few years.

Having this foundation established is important as you move into the next phase, *Create Hopeful Urgency* and *Chart a Course.* You'll want to refer back to your values, purpose, and vision as you work. In our experience, leaders and leadership teams that enact—truly live—their school's values and purpose on a daily basis find decision making becomes easier when everyone understands this foundation. The first question they ask when faced with a challenging situation or need for action is, "Is this consistent with what we believe?" If the answer is yes, they advance their process; if the answer is no, they are able to ground their decision in their beliefs.

Phase 2.1: Create Hopeful Urgency

What are we doing right . . . and what must we do to be better?

A Curious New Direction Emerges

Over what seemed like a short summer, each member of the Stillbrook K–8 leadership team read a stack of books and articles. They sent many emails back and forth and occasionally met to talk over what they were learning and share ideas about how to get their school unstuck. So, when they sat down for their first official leadership meeting of the year in early August, they were ready to volunteer observations about why their school had gotten "stuck." After generating a lengthy list on a whiteboard, Janice asked everyone to put a star next to three ideas that most resonated with them. These ideas emerged:

- *Our kids are disengaged/bored.*

- *It's been a few years since we've seen real gains in achievement. Are we losing our will?*

- *Writing scores still low; kids can read, but don't know how to THINK.*

- *Instructional quality uneven — mix of novice teachers and some veterans who have "checked out."*

- *Too many distractions — from district, state, parents.*

Tom Green, the science teacher and instructional coach, summed up the list. "I think it all comes down to teaching and learning. But with everything that's been going on with the new standards and district stuff and drama around the PTA coup d'état, it seems like we've kind of lost our focus."

Janice agreed, and asked Tom to describe what seemed to be missing in the classrooms he visited.

He shrugged. "Mostly, I think we just have a lot of teachers who are burned out and just going through the motions; they're doing things without really knowing *why*. In one class, the kids spent two weeks making a periodic table out of cereal boxes. It was supposed to be engaging, but I had no idea — nor did the teacher *or students* for that matter — what the kids were actually *learning*. That doesn't seem like real engagement to me."

The others nodded in agreement.

"So where should we begin?" Janice asked.

"With curiosity," offered Belinda Gray, a 4th-grade teacher who also served as a coach for primary grade teachers. Everyone knew her to be an amazing teacher. When she spoke, people listened. Seeing the others' quizzical looks, she continued. "I picked up a book on it this summer — well, two actually. One led to the other. I got *curious*, I guess," she added with a smile. Belinda shared what she learned about curiosity — how it led to better learning, career outcomes, relationships, and life satisfaction — and how it was quashed in a lot of schools, like Stillbrook.

"To be fair," Belinda added, "I think we *do* cultivate curiosity in things like our after-school robotics program and the great figures in history poetry slam we did last year. We just don't do it very often in our regular classrooms."

The rest of the group agreed and then, during a brief conversation, reflected on many other things Stillbrook had gotten *right:* It was a safe school, parents were involved, they had good teachers and good after-school programs. "We beat ourselves up a lot, but we're a pretty good school," said Tom.

"But not great," Janice interjected.

"And that's how we'll get better," chimed in Oscar, the introspective assistant principal who had been mostly silent up to this point.

"You sound like an inspirational poster," quipped Belinda, the primary grades instructional coach. "We get *better* by seeing that we're only *good*, yet want to be *great*."

Janice smiled and wrote the phrase on the whiteboard. Soon, they had a focus—one that energized them. They would help teachers become more intentional in their practice, so in turn, they could help students become more *curious* as learners.

"What I like about this," said Tom, "is that it's *fresh*. It's not doing the same thing and expecting different results. It's a whole new way of looking at the challenges we're facing. We're not just trying to boost test scores or push kids from one performance band to the next; we're trying to get kids *excited* about their learning. And who could argue with that?"

"Well, I can think of a few people," Belinda quipped, an oblique reference to the cabal of curmudgeonly parents who had drummed a well-liked parent off the PTA.

Janice gently chided them. "Now, now. Who knows? The idea of curiosity might even bring them around. And by the way, I *already* see student curiosity in some of the classrooms I visit, like Belinda's. So, while it may stretch us in some ways, I think we can do this. But, let me ask you this. I love the idea of curiosity. Seeing kids and teachers abuzz with a desire to learn—that sounds amazing. But is it too

grandiose?" she asked, moving deftly from leader to devil's advocate.

"Well, I *like* that it's grandiose," said Oscar. "Like Tom, I get worried when I hear people fixating on test scores as the be-all-end-all. I mean, let's talk about *learning*—the important stuff. I think we're all worn out from working so hard and not seeing any results. So, we need something big to inspire us. That's what I like about this whole curiosity thing. But it can't be just one more thing we're doing; it's got to be THE thing that really brings us together."

"I totally agree," said Tom. "Of course, I'm still not sure what the thing *is*. Is it a new curriculum, new lesson plans, new teaching strategies, a new culture in the school . . . or all of the above? I want us to move ahead with this; I'm just not sure what it's going to look like."

Oscar pondered that for a few seconds before saying, "Well, maybe that's OK. Look, even though we're the leadership team, we don't need to have *all* the answers. Maybe that's gotten us into trouble in the past—assuming we have the answers and dictating where we're going. Maybe *we* should be what we want our kids to be: *curious.* We should see ourselves as a Research and Innovation Team. OK, I got that from something I read this summer. But let's talk to everyone in the school about our vision and what it should mean for our school—how we might work together differently to meet every kid where they are and unleash the curiosity that Belinda so eloquently told us is bottled up inside them."

"And let's also ask people what they're *already doing* to help kids be curious," Belinda interjected. "Let's do this from a glass-half-full perspective."

Janice looked around at the nodding heads in the room before declaring, "That sounds like a good place to begin." ■

Creating Hope for a Brighter Future

With a foundation of values, purpose, and vision in place, you're ready to dive deeper and paint an even more specific picture of where your school is headed—*together*.

A research team at McREL set out to determine how high-poverty, high-performing, "beat-the-odds" schools differ from low-performing schools in matched comparison studies (McREL, 2005). The team asked several hundred teachers in high-poverty, high- and low-performing schools to rate how well their schools addressed many key correlates of school performance, including these:

- My school has an explicit statement of high expectations concerning student achievement.

- There is a safe, orderly learning environment in my school.

- Administrators, teachers, and parents share a common vision of school improvement.

- My students know their learning goals.

Some surprising differences emerged in what teachers in low-performing schools said *wasn't* happening in their schools, namely a constellation of elements that appeared to add up to a different, better kind of school *culture* (see sidebar). Unlike low-performing schools, beat-the-odds schools had developed, with input from teachers, a *common vision* grounded in a belief that all students can learn. Notably, teachers reported having influence in school decisions; they shared the vision and owned the success of the school.

> **Distinguishing characteristics of beat-the-odds schools**
>
> - Shared mission and goals (*common vision and clear focus for resources*)
> - Academic press for achievement (*high expectations for all*)
> - Orderly climate (*clear and enforced rules for student behavior*)
> - Support for teacher influence (*leadership shared with teachers*)
> - Structure (*clear student goals, strong classroom management*)

As you already know, a vision starts with where your school is now and paints a picture of where you want it to be. Your leadership team (or RIT), of course, plays a key role in shaping and sharing this vision. In fact, in its research on effective leaders, McREL identified two key responsibilities of effective leaders that apply here:

- Inspiring people to innovate and take on challenges that may seem initially beyond their reach (helping to "optimize" performance).

- Challenging the status quo by reframing change not as a loss, but as a gain, moving everyone toward a better future (operating as a "change agent").

You've already drafted a vision; now it's time to leverage your school's data to shape the vision into tangible outcomes that matter to everyone in your community. To do this, you need to look honestly and openly at what you know about your school—challenges *and* strengths—and agree on what should be maintained and strengthened, and what needs to change. Effective school leaders frequently use unsatisfactory data, changing conditions, or hope for a better future to create *discontent with the current reality* while helping people *picture a more attractive reality.* That is, they use their school's data to portray an accurate picture of their current status, and build optimism by helping everyone believe that a brighter future is possible. This doesn't mean frightening everyone into thinking the sky is falling. Rather, it's creating a sense of urgency and making the status quo no longer acceptable.

By creating a chasm between the current reality and a preferred future, leaders motivate people to move beyond the status quo. These same leaders also point to bright spots in their school's data and practices to illustrate what is possible.

The tool on the following two pages is designed to help you and your RIT shape your vision into tangible outcomes that matter to all.

Tool #4: Data springboard

We often want to use data and facts to frighten people into seeking a better future. However, most people are more motivated by a sense of compassion and purpose. This tool will help you dive deeply into your data through the lens of your moral purpose to create discontent with the current reality while instilling hope for a better future.

1. In the space below or on a separate piece of paper, briefly describe your current reality using multiple types of data, including the following:

    Demographic data are simple descriptors of your school, such as enrollment, student attendance, or teacher qualifications (e.g., 22% of our students are enrolled in AP classes, our average daily attendance rate is 92%, a quarter of our teachers will retire in five years). You might call out trends in these data (e.g., enrollment in AP classes is declining).

    Perception data provide information about how various members of your community (e.g., parents, teachers, or students) feel about how your school is operating or the direction it might go (e.g., 67% of parents report our school is "good or very good" at meeting their children's needs, 60% of our students report their classes are "boring" or "not challenging"). You'll want to be sure you have—or plan to collect—perception data that represents the various stakeholders and student populations in your school.

    Performance data typically include *achievement data* (e.g., state assessments, curriculum-based assessments, benchmark assessments, end-of-course grades, and/or grade point averages) as well as *outcomes data* which give final results or conclusions for students, including graduation rates, dropout rates, mobility rates, suspensions/expulsions, intervention exit rates, and postsecondary acceptance. As with perception data, it's important to examine multiple data points as well as trends and discrepancies among different groups of students.

    Program data describe how educational programs are conducted in a school, district, or other organization (e.g., textbooks used, professional learning opportunities for teachers, graduation requirements and course offerings, instructional strategies used, and extracurricular activities and educational opportunities for students).

2. Think about what your team identified as your school's purpose and vision. Do your data reflect your aspirations for students? Identify where your data and your purpose and vision diverge (e.g., "Knowing that we define engagement as participation *and* learning, these student engagement rates are unacceptable for a school that aspires to engage all learners").

3. In the space below or on a separate piece of paper, paint a picture of what your school would look like if these data were dramatically different. Start with this prompt: Imagine three years from now that these data are off-the-charts excellent (e.g., 100% of students report feeling engaged every day).

   - What will have changed for students?

   - What will have changed about teaching and learning?

   - What will a perfect day of school look like?

   - How will we feel about ourselves and our students?

   - What will have changed about us as an organization?

   - What other (even less tangible) benefits might we experience?

While data can help to create urgency to improve your current reality, your focus here is to understand your current status and become more specific in your vision, as you appeal to people's deeper sense of purpose and imagination. Thus, it's not about hitting numbers (e.g., improving test scores by 3 points), but doing the right thing for others and creating a new, better reality.

Turn to page 101 and follow the ToolTracker prompts to capture a data-informed picture of your school's current reality.

Seeing the Glass Half Full: What's Working?

With a clear picture of reality, thanks to your dive into your data and a growing urgency about your school's purpose and vision, it's time to turn our attention to, and celebrate, those things that you're already doing to change the odds for your students.

In a famed experiment gone awry, psychologist Martin Seligman (1990) inadvertently "taught" dogs to feel helpless. By trapping them in a crate while giving them a mild shock (equivalent to static discharge), he'd hoped to condition them to associate a bell tone with the shock, but instead taught them "that nothing they did mattered. So why try?" (p. 20). Seligman realized that downtrodden people also exhibit a similar behavior, what he called "learned helplessness," which is often a matter of how they interpret events. Do they, for example, view a disappointing result as a temporary setback or as a permanent reflection of their inadequacies? Do they see failure as an indication that *everything* must be wrong or as opportunities to do things better the next time?

School researchers also have found that "in the same way individuals can develop learned helplessness, organizations can be seduced by pervasive pessimism" (Hoy, Tarter, & Hoy, 2006, p. 440). School teams come to believe that their students can't learn and there's nothing they can do about it, so why bother? In demoralized schools, even the simplest solution—such as adopting a reading program that's been shown to be successful in other schools—tends to have little impact. High-performing schools, on the other hand, demonstrate a different attitude: something akin to *academic optimism*, or seeing "teachers as capable, students as willing, parents as supportive, and the task as achievable" (p. 440).

Thus, how leaders explain successes and interpret failures has a powerful influence on their schools. Do leaders attribute declining performance to external (or universal) factors over which people have no control (e.g., changing demographics of their school population)? If so, they'll likely encourage learned helplessness, convincing people their actions are futile. If, on the other hand, they look for specific causes for the problem (e.g., not providing adequate early interventions for reading), they can help people develop *academic optimism*.

Leaders can also foster optimism in their schools by employing *asset-based thinking*— purposefully viewing what could be seen as a challenge or weakness as a strength or opportunity instead. Indeed, a common feature of high-performing schools is that instead of dwelling on perceived deficits in students, they recognize and build upon the many strengths students bring to school, such as family aspirations, bilingualism, extended families, and resilience (Yosso, 2005).

Table 1 below provides some additional examples of how asset-based thinking can help to translate perceived challenges or weaknesses into opportunities and strengths.

Table 1. Examples of translating deficits into assets

Deficit thinking	Asset-based thinking
Our students are ELLs.	Our students are multilingual.
Our parents are immigrants.	Our parents bring a wealth of experiences.
Our teachers are young and ineffective.	They're spirited and eager to learn.
Our teachers are old and set in their ways.	They're experienced with good ideas.
Our building is old and falling apart.	We have a strong history and traditions.
We don't have enough resources.	Necessity is the mother of invention!
The district doesn't pay attention to us.	The district gives us latitude to innovate.
We have a lot of behavior issues.	We have opportunities to teach character.

We all have a natural tendency to focus on what's wrong when engaged in improvement planning—our achievement gaps, our students' learning needs, our lack of knowledge and skills. Yet fixating too much on what's wrong can lead to deficit-minded thinking or learned helplessness. Thus, at the same time that we examine the data that generates discontent, it's important to take time to identify what's going right in your school. You may be surprised to see that quite often, the answers and solutions to many of your challenges are there, right in front of your eyes.

The tool on the following page will help you and your colleagues further develop asset-based thinking in your school.

Tool #5: Applying asset-based thinking to school challenges

This exercise asks you and your colleagues to look for five positive aspects of your school for every negative one.

1. Pick a data point that is challenging for your school. It could be quantitative data, like test scores, or observational data about, for example, student behavior. Write it in the large circle.

2. Now, identify five positive elements related to that same data point. For example, if you find many students are below proficient in mathematics, you might identify which standards they *have* mastered, which students are making rapid progress, and in which classrooms they're having success. Be specific.

3. Next, consider how this positive outcome came about. What did you do to create it? (It's important to attribute the positive result to a perceived strength or some action you've taken.)

4. Next, look for common themes in your strengths and the actions you've taken. What do you notice?

5. Look across these strengths and identify those that might be applied in other situations. Create a list of strengths to leverage and actions to "scale up" or replicate. For example, if some students have experienced success in their science classes after participating in sessions introducing academic and content vocabulary prior to class, you might consider whether this is a model that could be scaled up and applied to other subjects.

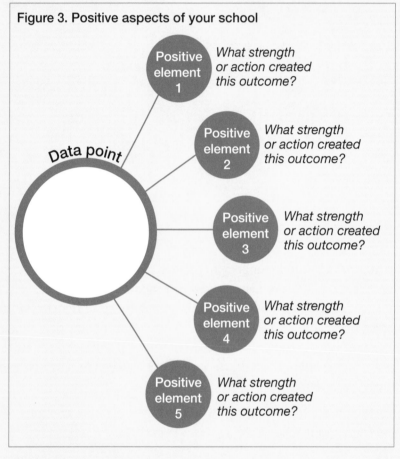

Figure 3. Positive aspects of your school

Data point

Positive element 1 — *What strength or action created this outcome?*

Positive element 2 — *What strength or action created this outcome?*

Positive element 3 — *What strength or action created this outcome?*

Positive element 4 — *What strength or action created this outcome?*

Positive element 5 — *What strength or action created this outcome?*

This last step is important because this is not intended to be an "I'm OK, you're OK" exercise that glosses over challenges and needs in your school. Rather, it's designed to energize your team by building a sense of "collective efficacy"—a sense that together, you can accomplish great things. In the next section, you'll extend this idea and build collective efficacy by looking for bright spots in your school using an instructional rounds process.

Use the ToolTracker on page 102 to bring your ideas from this tool together.

Looking for and Building on Bright Spots

As noted, it's essential to look at data that help us understand where our school is vulnerable or struggling. And, as illustrated in the previous section, we also need to examine those elements of our school that work well. In their book *Switch*, Chip and Dan Heath (2010) recount the story of Jerry Sternin, an aid worker for Save the Children who was dispatched to Vietnam to help local villagers combat child malnutrition. The problem, initially, seemed intractable—the result of grinding poverty and lack of education. When faced with big challenges like that, people tend to dive deeply into the problem in hopes of figuring out how to fix it.

Sternin, however, took a different approach. He traveled to local villages, brought people together, and asked them to weigh their children in hopes of finding a handful of children from impoverished families who *weren't* malnourished. He then observed those families closely to see what they were doing differently and uncovered a surprising insight: Rather than feeding infants twice a day, as was common, mothers of healthy children fed them the same amount of food, but as smaller meals four times a day with tiny discarded pieces of shrimp and crawfish mixed in. As a result, their children were better able to digest the smaller meals and they got additional protein to help them grow.

By hitting upon a "bright spot"—what researchers call "positive deviants" or outliers—Sternin was able to share a credible, simple solution for addressing malnutrition among the other children in those villages.

Schools can do the same thing. For example, in northern Melbourne, Australia, educators went on a scavenger hunt for bright spots—classrooms where students were highly engaged in rigorous learning. They used instructional rounds, a non-evaluative classroom observation protocol developed by Elizabeth City, Richard Elmore, and their colleagues at Harvard (City, Elmore, Fiarman, & Teitel, 2009) that was already prevalent in Victoria to get teams of teachers to visit one another's classrooms. This was not done in a finger-wagging way to see what they were doing *wrong*, but rather, to uncover what they were doing *right*. That is, they purposely sought to identify the best practices of effective teachers that *already existed* in schools that support student literacy, numeracy, and curiosity. Afterward, they synthesized what they had observed in the classrooms of highly effective teachers into six key practices that were shared with teachers across the region. Because they were drawn from real-life examples and grounded in research, teachers found them to be straightforward and easy to apply in their own classrooms.

Finding and building on bright spots is a powerful way to improve practice because it doesn't feel abstract, far-fetched, or mismatched to students. Moreover, we know from research that so-called vicarious experiences are important motivators; when we can see someone else doing (and having success with) what's being asked of us, we're far more likely to believe that we can be successful and to try it ourselves, especially if we view the other person as like us (Bandura, 1977, 1986, 1997).

The tool on the next page can help you and your colleagues use instructional rounds to surface best practices that already exist in your classrooms, which, if used more consistently in other classrooms, could help you address your critical challenges.

Two caveats:

1. Don't limit yourself to looking for a predetermined list of teacher or student actions; the purpose of this exercise is to observe themes across your school that can create a local definition of successful teaching and learning.

2. Don't confuse this process with evaluation or monitoring; remember, you're looking for bright spots.

What are *instructional rounds*?

Instructional rounds are brief observations of classrooms during teaching and learning. Sometimes called "walkthroughs," instructional rounds can be done by peer teachers, coaches, or members of a school leadership team. The goal is not evaluation of the teacher. Instead, the goal should be to discover, and later reflect on and share, "bright spots" and best practices—things that are going really well in one classroom that could be used or adapted in others. Rounds are best done in small groups, just 2–3 people observing a classroom for about 10–15 minutes, with as little disruption as possible to the teaching and learning.

Tool #6: Using instructional rounds to find bright spots

1. Identify someone to lead the rounds process, ideally a lead teacher or well-respected teacher.

2. Select 3–5 people for each group that will be conducting rounds.

3. Communicate clearly up-front to everyone—observers and teachers being observed—that the goal of the process is *non-evaluative.* You're looking for bright spots, not problems.

4. Let everyone know in advance which days the group will be visiting their classrooms, so they can prepare their students beforehand.

5. Upon arriving in the classroom, move to the back or out of the way. Then simply and quietly observe the classroom for 10–15 minutes.

6. The group can either identify a focus for their visits (e.g., student engagement, student-teacher interactions) or simply make mental or written notes on what they see as bright spots (e.g., on-task behaviors, effective teaching strategies). Avoid using rubrics or scoring sheets. Remember, teams are just looking for things that can help them improve their own practices or, in a general way, other teachers' practices.

7. After 3–4 classroom visits, groups debrief on what they saw. We suggest generating a list of positives (!) and questions (?)—things observers might wonder about or want to know more about (e.g., why a teacher selected a certain strategy). Remember, the purpose is to look for bright spots, not to nitpick teachers.

8. Observers should share their *affirmations*—strategies already in use that they want to keep using (e.g., wait time); *reflections*—strategies they currently use that they might want to reconsider (e.g., calling on students with raised hands); and *considerations*—strategies they observed that they'd like to try in their own classrooms (e.g., calling on students randomly).

9. Finally, the entire group should engage in discussion about the conditions needed to replicate the bright spots. Being curious about and understanding the precursors to success will help everyone consider what's needed to effectively implement some of the practices they observed. Discussion-starters might sound like, "What did Mr. Rivera do to support his students in being able to engage in robust, on-task, student-to-student talk?" or "Ms. Painter, Mr. Thomas, and the entire 3rd-grade team all asked questions that really stimulated discussion and curiosity. How did they learn how to ask those 'just right' questions?" The team likely will discover that there is more to these practices than simply applying an instructional strategy—and that's how bright spots can catalyze an inquiry-driven learning process for teachers.

10. Make a list of five key messages you'd like everyone in your community to know about your school. Be sure to include challenges *and* bright spots.

Use the ToolTracker on page 103 to capture your reflections about the bright spots you identified during instructional rounds. Be sure to add notes about the evidence team members observed that qualifies your bright spots as strengths.

Sit back for a moment and consider what you've accomplished on this journey so far. School improvement and innovation is important work; time focused on your school's foundation (values, purpose, vision) and current status is time well spent. Before we move forward, we recommend you take a few minutes to reflect on the following:

- Read your values, purpose, and vision statements aloud. Now that you've had time to think more deeply about your school's challenges and bright spots, make any minor revisions.

- Review what you learned (or were reminded of) from your school's data.

- As an RIT, be sure you agree on where you're headed. Remember, you're only talking about where you've been, where you're going, and why you're going there. You don't have to figure out how you'll get there yet.

Phase 2 can be intense, so take a collective deep breath. Next, we're going to help you focus on where to begin so you can get to work. But first, let's find out what the team at Stillbrook K–8 School is talking about.

Phase 2.2: Chart a Course

Where do we start our journey?

Avoiding Hallucinations: Turning a Vision into a Plan

During a lively session in late August, a vision began to emerge for the Stillbrook K–8 School leadership team (now called the Research and Innovation Team or RIT) about the kind of school they wanted to be: a place full of joyful learning with intellectual surprises around every corner. It would be a place where everyone *couldn't wait* to come to school because students would be fully engaged in learning and teachers would be expert practitioners piquing their curiosity and guiding their learning. Belinda drew a picture of a hot air balloon on the whiteboard and added the words "Curiosity" in the balloon and "Learning" in the basket. The image stuck, along with the phrase, "Curiosity lifting all learners."

They also began to see curiosity everywhere they looked. Tom saw it in his 99-year-old grandfather, who kept his mind active by reading news magazines and history books from cover to cover. Oscar delighted in his young daughter's curiosity during their walks in the park. And Belinda had found small ways to spark her students' curiosity in the classroom and was amazed at the difference it was already making in their engagement.

Tom and Belinda had also introduced the idea of curiosity to their fellow teachers, who were almost unanimously excited about it—and curious themselves. Many teachers offered ideas for what they were already doing to create curiosity and how they might encourage even more of it among their students. And some, like Belinda and Tom, had already begun engaging in small, curiosity-stoking experiments in their classrooms.

However, when Janice walked into an RIT meeting in early September, her brow was furrowed. Tom noticed her look of concern right away. "What's on your mind, boss?" he asked.

"Well, I've always been a take-charge kind of leader," she said slowly, "and this feels very different to me. I love that we have a clear sense of purpose and a shared vision, but I feel like we don't have much of a *plan*. Who was it that said, 'A vision without a plan is just a hallucination'?"

The group laughed nervously.

"That became apparent to me when I tried to explain what we're doing to people downtown in the central office and to the new group on the PTA," Janice continued. "Don't get me wrong: I love the energy I'm seeing. But it feels messy, bordering on chaotic. What's keeping me awake at night right now is worrying how we're going to achieve the kind of consistency in teaching quality we need. And if the wheels come off all of this excitement, and our test scores slump, well, I'm going to have some explaining to do."

Janice's comments hung in the air for several seconds before Oscar finally spoke. "I think we need to embrace the messiness to some extent. We need to experiment and figure things out together; it will be more meaningful and powerful when we do. But I agree, we need a tighter *focus* for our efforts. At least I'm pretty sure we'll be better off doing a few things well than a bunch of things poorly, no matter how cool they might be."

"I hear what you're saying," Belinda offered. "It's like we're trying to transition from being a marching band to more of a jazz band, where we improvise and experiment with things, but are still playing from the same sheet of music."

"That's a nice way of putting it," Janice replied. "So I guess I'm asking, what is that sheet of music? What strategies will we work on together to help kids become more curious? I want to make sure that we don't let all the good things we've put in place over the last several years, like our pacing guides and bell-ringers and lesson plan templates, unravel."

"So that we *build on*, not dismantle, everything we've done so far," Tom offered.

"Yes, precisely," said Janice. "How can we make sure whatever we're doing here feels like a step *forward* and not backtracking on our hard work—the things that got us to this point?"

"It's as if we need a way to look at the big picture of what we've done so far, and then decide, together, where we ought to go from here," Oscar said.

Janice smiled at her assistant principal's knack for sizing things up and figuring out what is needed. "Exactly," she replied. "Do you have any ideas about how we might do that?"

Oscar nodded slowly. "Well, maybe. It's something I came across at a conference that might be helpful," he said, pulling out a large chart from a folder. "Let me introduce you to a pathway of improvement." ∎

Assessing Your Progress Toward Innovation

Where to focus?

That's a key question for many school leadership teams. Often, school improvement plans call upon people to do too many things at once, and as a result, they are overwhelmed or unsure of where to focus, and end up doing little well.

This part of the process will help you find a clear focus for your efforts by looking at your progress using research-based leverage points for student success and your school's current position along a continuum that stretches from establishing key routines to fostering shared innovation.

Looking at your school through these two lenses can profoundly change how you view improvement and innovation and where to focus your efforts, so we'll examine each more fully. As you read about these two lenses, keep your ToolTracker close at hand; you'll want to refer to it as you think about your focus.

Focusing on What Matters Most

As explained in greater detail in the book, *Simply Better: Doing What Matters Most to Change the Odds for Student Success* (Goodwin, 2011), McREL identified, through an extensive synthesis of hundreds of research reports, the five key leverage points for school and system improvement efforts, illustrated in Figure 4 below.

Since the 1970s, we've known the *correlates* of effective schools—what distinguishes higher-performing schools from lower-performing ones. It's helpful to know the "end state" of effective schools, of course. Yet simply knowing the attributes of high-performing schools doesn't answer the questions most school leaders and leadership teams ask themselves: *How* exactly do schools improve? Where do they begin? And where do they focus their limited time and energy (what "levers" do they pull) to most efficiently improve student outcomes?

Figure 4. What Matters Most® framework

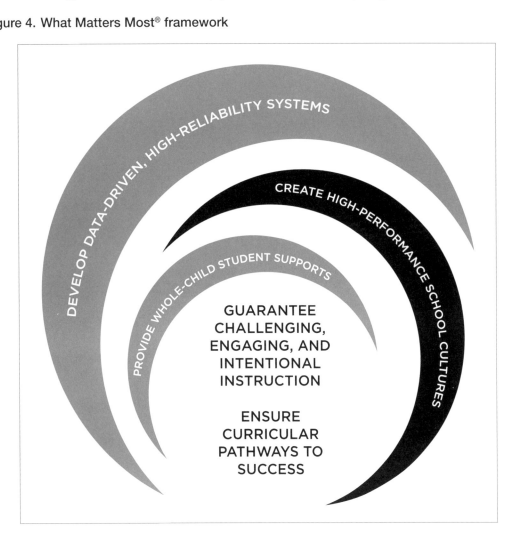

The answers from research are the five components of the What Matters Most framework, described in Table 2.

Table 2. What Matters Most component descriptions

What Matters Most component	Description
Curricular pathways to success	High-performing systems guarantee that every student in every classroom—no matter what their aspirations are—is provided with challenging and personalized learning experiences that prepare each of them for life success.
Challenging, engaging, and intentional instruction	At the core of effective systems are teachers who challenge students, develop positive relationships with them, and are intentional in their use of a broad repertoire of teaching strategies.
Whole-child student supports	Setting high expectations requires providing students with the scaffolding they need to succeed—a just-in-time, personalized response to students' cognitive, social-emotional, and academic needs.
High-performance school cultures	Effective schools ensure high-quality learning experiences in every classroom. At the same time, they develop a culture of high expectations for learning and behavior, which is an even more powerful predictor of student success than socioeconomic status.
Data-driven, high-reliability systems	High-performing school systems put reliable, consistently used data systems and processes in place to ensure high-quality learning experiences for all students, as well as real-time responses to student struggles.

Understanding the Stages of Improvement

A second major insight drawn from research is that while school contexts may vary, the stages of development on the journey to innovation look remarkably similar from school to school (Barber & Mourshed, 2007), reflecting these four stages:

- **Adopt better routines**. The key difference between high- and low-performing schools is summed up in one word: *consistency*. Thus, the first thing schools must do as they improve and move toward innovation is focus on adopting better routines to increase the quality—and reduce the variability—in core elements of teaching and learning. Often this takes the form of clearly articulating their curriculum and establishing a model for instruction—a blueprint that shows teachers how to design and deliver instruction.

- **Ensure greater consistency**. The second phase of improvement grows out of the first; it focuses on ensuring consistent implementation of the better routines to guarantee that all students benefit from high-quality learning environments. Often when schools are in these first two phases of development, many students are falling through the cracks, which creates a great deal of urgency and the need to move fast. As a result, school leadership teams may find themselves operating in more of a top-down, or outside-in, manner to gain momentum and realize small wins.

- **Develop collegial expertise**. Better routines, however, are simply that: *better*, but not yet perfect. Consistently implementing better routines (e.g., a set of research-based instructional strategies) will often bring significant initial gains. Yet even the best strategies won't work for all students, all the time. It's at this point that many schools get stuck looking for new strategies or ratcheting up the outside-in pressure, when what's needed is professional expertise—for example, teachers learning to use data to guide instruction and address student learning needs. Because we cannot force expertise on anyone, schools in this stage must pivot to *inside-out* approaches and professional capacity building as shown in Figure 5 on page 38. It's in this stage also where the shift from "prescription" to "precision" really begins to take hold, as teachers adapt best practices to more precisely meet the needs of their students.

- **Foster shared innovation**. Ultimately, creating learning environments where curiosity can flourish requires complex approaches like inquiry-based learning or personalized learning. Schools that create such learning environments adopt a fail-fast and fail-forward ethos, using data to engage in rapid-cycle innovation efforts. Teachers and students aren't left to their own devices, but continue to learn together and share their innovative approaches with one another (e.g., identifying "learning competencies" and data systems to guide student learning) to ensure the entire system benefits from the innovations.

There's no need for teachers to abandon all of the consistent practices and schoolwide protocols that contributed to their success so far. Innovation is a balance between maintaining those structures, systems, and approaches that are foundational to how the school functions, and creating and testing new ideas to achieve better results that are aligned with the school's purpose and vision.

Figure 5. Stages of improvement: Pivoting from external to internal accountability

| Intervention · · · · · · · Building Capacity and Professional Practice · · · · · ▶ Innovation |

EXTERNAL ACCOUNTABILITY
Top-down, or outside-in, intervention

INTERNAL ACCOUNTABILITY
Bottom-up, or inside-out, innovation

| Adopt better routines | Ensure greater consistency | Develop collegial expertise | Foster shared innovation |

| Intervention · · · · · · · · · · · System Leadership and Support · · · · · · · · · ▶ Innovation |

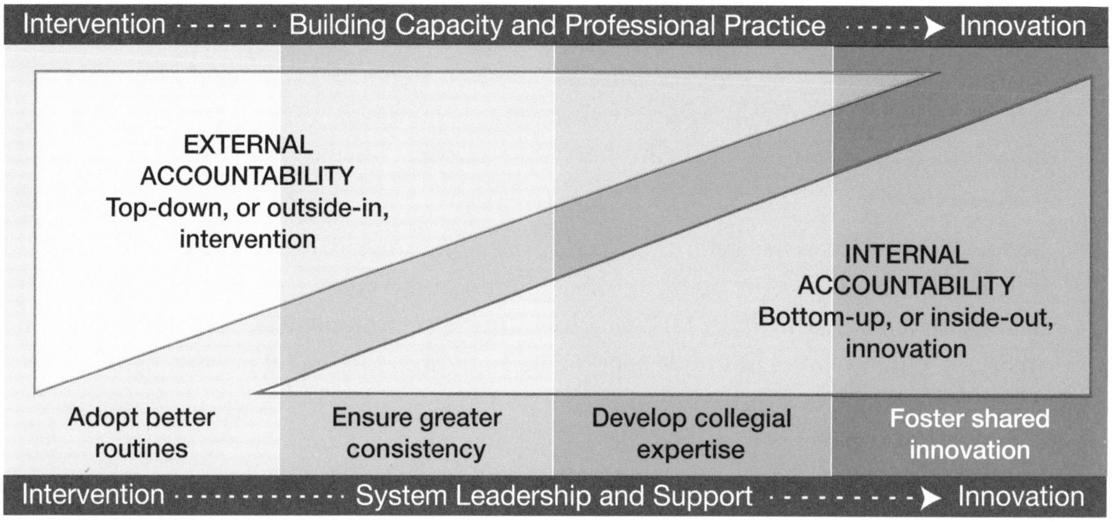

The improvement and innovation pathways tools you'll find on the next several pages bring the content of the What Matters Most framework together with the stages of improvement. We'll walk you through a process that will help you and your colleagues take stock of your school's journey to date and develop a clear picture of where your focus should be over the next few years, and most important, in the next 9–12 months.

In short, these next three tools will guide you through a conversation to identify what matters most to *your* school *right now*.

Tool #7: What Matters Most improvement and innovation pathways

Choose one of the What Matters Most framework components (see Table 2 on page 36) as a starting point. Select one that resonates with your team, whether it's an area that's been a recent focus or one you haven't considered lately.

Then, using the school improvement and innovation pathways on pages 40–44 that are matched to the What Matters Most framework, you and your colleagues will identify where your school is along a continuum of improvement and begin to select a focus for your school improvement and innovation efforts.

Read the pathway document carefully and annotate. Each member of the team should read the descriptors in each column. Use an agreed-upon annotation system as you read. For example:

★ Bright spots—things you think your school does well

▲ Learn more—not sure if we do this

! Not there yet—could be an area for improvement

Pay attention to the column headings. Remember, you're seeking to describe your school *as a whole.* So if you say, "Some teachers do that well" or "The math team is good at that," but can't say, "Nearly all of our teachers do that" or "We do that across our school," then the columns to the left of that spot on the pathway likely best describe your school. The goal isn't to exaggerate your position on the pathway, but rather, to engage in a thoughtful assessment of your strengths and opportunities, increase consistency, and move toward expertise and innovation. You may find your school fits descriptions in more than one column. That's OK! Your goal is to get a big picture of your school's journey toward innovation, including its current bright spots and areas for growth.

Share your observations. After everyone has read the pathway, each person shares what they see as your school's bright spots, what they're curious and want to learn more about, and one or two possible areas for improvement. This is an opportunity to hear different perspectives. You'll consider evidence in the next step.

Consider the data points that support your assessment. Begin with bright spots. What data support them? This is where you can consider consistency. Do the data reflect *all classrooms*, or just a few? Bright spots that occur in one or only a few places serve as models for what you'd like to see across the school. As you discuss your bright spots, you might find you don't have data to support some of your assumptions; that's not uncommon. Make a note to collect additional evidence to support your beliefs about where your school is shining.

Look across the entire pathway. Where along the pathway have you identified bright spots? Do they tend to cluster in one column (stage)? Are they spread across the stages? Re-read the descriptions for each stage. Which one sounds the most like your school? As a team, come to consensus on the stage that best represents where your school is on that pathway component.
This is where you'll position your school on this pathway.

With one pathway reviewed, move on to the next, until you've completed all five. Take your time with this important step.

When you've completed this step, turn to the ToolTracker on pages 104–105 to record information from this self-assessment. You'll find space to indicate where you think your school is along each pathway, as well as room to list bright spots, areas for growth, and data that will help complete your story.

School Improvement and Innovation Pathways | What Matters Most Component:
Curricular Pathways to Success

Adopt Better Routines	Ensure Greater Consistency	Develop Collegial Expertise	Foster Shared Innovation
Improvement begins by identifying and adopting research-based best practices, even though some inconsistencies and lack of stakeholder buy-in may remain.	*Best practices become standardized by focusing on buy-in and fidelity of implementation, yet professional knowledge remains limited.*	*Consistent routines are enhanced with collegial learning that supports "precision without prescription," yet with limited innovation.*	*High levels of staff expertise support an entrepreneurial culture that uses rapid-cycle innovation to develop and share improved routines.*
We articulate a strong press for achievement and the need for all students to have opportunities to learn challenging content. We have translated our expectations for student learning into a clearly articulated and focused ("viable") curriculum that is vertically aligned and reflects rigorous standards for learning and high expectations for students. We have provided teachers with tools (e.g., curriculum/ pacing guides, model lessons, common assessments) to support their use of curriculum in classrooms.	Our teachers consistently use our adopted common curriculum/program in daily classroom activities. Our leaders regularly monitor use of curriculum in classrooms to ensure our curriculum is "guaranteed," giving all students, regardless of their classroom assignment, opportunities to learn challenging content. To avoid curriculum "creep" or misalignment, we regularly discuss curriculum articulation across grade levels and courses during our professional learning or faculty meetings.	To ensure our curriculum motivates and addresses the needs of all learners, our teachers collaboratively review, enhance, and adapt the curriculum, developing shared resources for learners at all performance levels. Through peer collaboration, we ensure consistent implementation of adaptations to our curriculum in all classrooms. On a regular (e.g., semi-annual) basis, we collaboratively engage in curriculum mapping to look for gaps, redundancies, or misalignments, and/ or to identify "big ideas" or essential questions to guide unit and lesson planning.	To ensure the success of every learner, we collaborate across our school and with other schools to create a variety of curricular pathways for students to demonstrate their learning while exploring their interests. Our teachers collaboratively develop curriculum innovations, studying and testing new ways to, for example, personalize student learning, monitor the effectiveness of new approaches, and incorporate them into practice, as appropriate. We use learner voice to guide enhancements to curriculum, designing learning for and with students.

School Improvement and Innovation Pathways | What Matters Most Component:
Challenging, Engaging, and Intentional Instruction

Adopt Better Routines	Ensure Greater Consistency	Develop Collegial Expertise	Foster Shared Innovation
Improvement begins by identifying and adopting research-based best practices, even though some inconsistencies and lack of stakeholder buy-in may remain.	*Best practices become standardized by focusing on buy-in and fidelity of implementation, yet professional knowledge remains limited.*	*Consistent routines are enhanced with collegial learning that supports "precision without prescription," yet with limited innovation.*	*High levels of staff expertise support an entrepreneurial culture that uses rapid-cycle innovation to develop and share improved routines.*
We have adopted a comprehensive model of instruction to guide the design of learning opportunities that challenge and engage students.

We have identified a set of research-informed instructional practices to support our instructional model and provide us with a shared professional vocabulary for discussing instructional strategies.

We provide exemplars (e.g., model lesson plans) and professional learning to help teachers use the instructional model in their classrooms. | We are committed to consistently using our instructional model and common research-informed instructional practices in every classroom.

Our teachers are committed to using research and best practices to enhance their pedagogical content knowledge and expand their repertoire of effective teaching strategies.

We ensure all our professional learning opportunities are explicitly designed and delivered to enhance application of our instructional model. | Our teachers understand effective teaching and the science of learning; they know what works and why it works and see (or re-frame) our instructional model as a learning model.

Our teachers collaboratively plan challenging learning tasks that meet students at their point of need, promoting curiosity, inquiry, and reflection.

We work together to collect, share, and analyze data to adjust teaching practices to meet student needs and expand our shared repertoire of research-based classroom practices. | Our teachers embrace assessment for learning and routinely study the impact of our instructional/learning model on student outcomes.

We use research, data, and best practice to continuously improve our learning/teaching model to meet the needs of all learners and reflect the collective wisdom of our teachers.

Our teachers embrace collaboration and use action research to develop innovative approaches to learning (e.g., technology enhanced, cross-curricular, personalized). |

School Improvement and Innovation Pathways | What Matters Most Component:
Whole-Child Student Supports

Adopt Better Routines	Ensure Greater Consistency	Develop Collegial Expertise	Foster Shared Innovation
Improvement begins by identifying and adopting research-based best practices, even though some inconsistencies and lack of stakeholder buy-in may remain.	*Best practices become standardized by focusing on buy-in and fidelity of implementation, yet professional knowledge remains limited.*	*Consistent routines are enhanced with collegial learning that supports "precision without prescription," yet with limited innovation.*	*High levels of staff expertise support an entrepreneurial culture that uses rapid-cycle innovation to develop and share improved routines.*
To ensure a safe and respectful environment, we have created behavioral expectations and communicated them to teachers, students, and parents. We have regular opportunities for teachers to discuss student learning and behavior with their families. We use a variety of methods to engage families in their students' learning. To catch students before they fall, we have systems to identify students who are struggling academically or emotionally and have processes in place to respond to student needs, including providing additional supports or connecting students and/or families with community resource options.	Our behavior expectations are translated into student-friendly language. We celebrate positive behavior and address infractions as opportunities to improve. We have developed positive relationships with students and families and provide regular feedback to students both about areas for improvement and bright spots in learning and behavior. We ensure no students fall through the cracks by consistently sharing information and observations about student learning progress and/or social-emotional needs with one another and support staff. As needed, we provide additional supports and services beyond the classroom or school.	We incorporate restorative practices into our behavior management program to build students' non-cognitive skills. We support their long-term success with a school-wide approach for emphasizing growth mindset, resilience, passion, persistence, and academic identity. Our teachers leverage strong student-teacher relationships and connections with families to discuss future pathways for development and work one-on-one with each student to develop personal plans for learning. Teachers are developing an increasingly deeper understanding of their own students' cognitive and non-cognitive challenges and use this knowledge to attend to their academic and non-academic needs and, when necessary, refer them to specialists and/or outside resources.	Students help create and teach our school's routines and procedures to peers. We seek student input as we engage in rapid-cycle development and testing of ways to create environments that build student non-cognitive and social-emotional skills. We scale up effective approaches school-wide. We are developing innovative systems for creating student profiles (including backgrounds and interests), helping students set goals for success, track progress, and receive real-time feedback from teachers on their progress. We have or are developing partnerships with external service providers on-site where they can connect with students, teachers, and families to discuss and address student needs, ensuring every student experiences success.

School Improvement and Innovation Pathways | What Matters Most Component:
High-Performance School Cultures

Adopt Better Routines	Ensure Greater Consistency	Develop Collegial Expertise	Foster Shared Innovation
Improvement begins by identifying and adopting research-based best practices, even though some inconsistencies and lack of stakeholder buy-in may remain.	*Best practices become standardized by focusing on buy-in and fidelity of implementation, yet professional knowledge remains limited.*	*Consistent routines are enhanced with collegial learning that supports "precision without prescription," yet with limited innovation.*	*High levels of staff expertise support an entrepreneurial culture that uses rapid-cycle innovation to develop and share improved routines.*
We communicate a press for achievement through our statement of school purpose.

We have identified and articulated core values for how we believe we should work together.

School leaders regularly visit classrooms to identify bright spots and opportunities for improvement.

We use staff meetings and teacher collaboration opportunities to share observations about student performance, best practice, and how teachers can improve.

We develop and share annual improvement plans with staff and use these plans to create shared focus and guide professional learning activities. | We clearly articulate a belief that all students can learn if we maintain a schoolwide focus on consistent, high-quality instructional practice in every classroom.

Our leaders embrace their role as instructional leaders and work directly with teachers to coach them toward better, more consistent professional practice.

Our school leaders understand that individuals respond differently to change and thus, monitor change efforts and support individuals who may need assistance through the process.

We regularly discuss school performance, celebrating success to build collective efficacy while staying focused on continuous improvement. | Collectively, we have developed a strong sense of shared, moral purpose and belief that every student can learn. Individually and collectively, we communicate high expectations for all students.

We reflect a community of learners by working together to help each other improve practice. Our teachers embrace peer coaching and developing precision without prescription by giving and receiving feedback and learning from bright spots in other classrooms.

Our school leaders create challenge, not threat, conditions, and model professional growth by connecting with other leaders in professional networks from which they draw insights, learn about best practice, and provide intellectual stimulation for staff. | We are committed to continuous improvement and constant examination of our practices to make them better.

Our leaders communicate and help us embrace a fail-forward ethos, letting staff know that it's OK to make mistakes as long as we learn from them. We engage in open dialogue about what's working and what's not.

We share our successes as a school community and highlight bright spots, while welcoming parent and student feedback on our school performance.

All staff participate in formal professional networks, as we believe we can learn from others and have an obligation to contribute to our profession. |

School Improvement and Innovation Pathways | What Matters Most Component:
Data-Driven, High-Reliability Systems

Adopt Better Routines	Ensure Greater Consistency	Develop Collegial Expertise	Foster Shared Innovation
Improvement begins by identifying and adopting research-based best practices, even though some inconsistencies and lack of stakeholder buy-in may remain.	*Best practices become standardized by focusing on buy-in and fidelity of implementation, yet professional knowledge remains limited.*	*Consistent routines are enhanced with collegial learning that supports "precision without prescription," yet with limited innovation.*	*High levels of staff expertise support an entrepreneurial culture that uses rapid-cycle innovation to develop and share improved routines.*
Our teachers collect and report data for compliance purposes. Our school leaders use data to inform decisions about school goals and professional learning. Our leaders embrace the need to operate as a high-reliability system and identify areas where structures and standard operating procedures are needed to ensure positive student outcomes. Our leaders understand the importance of teacher quality and use performance appraisals, feedback, and coaching conversations to recognize high performers, guide professional growth for all teachers, and, if necessary, remove low performers.	We use shared protocols for collecting and analyzing data on student outcomes and program implementation during regular data team meetings. Our leaders embrace their responsibility to monitor and evaluate schoolwide use of our curriculum and instruction model, conducting informal classroom observations and providing coaching feedback to support teachers' consistent use of these (and other) critical routines. Our leaders help us stay focused on finishing what we start by aligning school resources, professional development, use of school and class time, staff meetings, and rewards for teachers with our stated goals.	Increasingly, we collect and track a variety of data related to our goals, including student engagement and perceptions. Teacher input guides annual school improvement planning. We align resources by creating start-, stop-, and keep-doing lists. We immerse staff in data and provide them data-reflection and decision-making tools that encourage using data as a mirror to identify how we (not others) must change to produce desired outcomes for students. We demonstrate deference to expertise by providing regular opportunities for teacher teams to diagnose student challenges and identify solutions (often drawn from existing bright spots). Together, we track the results, develop precision of practice, and make necessary adjustments.	All staff regularly collect, analyze, and use a variety of data to make shared decisions about where we must improve and innovate to address adaptive challenges. To become a leading-edge school, our teachers guide their own professional learning, committing to staying abreast of their field and networking with others to identify next practice that will enhance our best practice and accelerate student learning. We have systematized innovation with agreed-upon process for rapid-cycle improvement, identifying needs, hypothesizing new solutions, testing results, and modifying solutions accordingly. Our leaders (and performance appraisals) recognize and reward teachers for developing expertise and applying next practices in their classrooms.

Tool #8: Finding your focus

Now that you've determined where your school is on each pathway, it's time to step back and look at everything you know about your school.

1. **Take a holistic snapshot of your school across all five pathways.**

    - Return to your data and the bright spots you identified through instructional rounds, and reconsider each pathway. Are there additional data you should consider?

    - Revisit the conditions you identified that allowed each bright spot to develop. How do those conditions align to the improvement stages and your snapshot assessment?

    - What story can you tell about your school using this information? Where have you been? What have you accomplished? What do you do well? Be sure to take stock of your current bright spots.

2. **Identify opportunities for growth.** Now, identify your school's opportunities for improvement and innovation—paying close attention to places where you've yet to adopt or ensure consistency in routines. Again, remind yourselves of the work you've done leading up to this point. Are there data points or bright spots identified earlier that need to be integrated into this discussion? Are there opportunities for growth that are especially well-aligned with your school's purpose and vision?

3. **As a team, develop a shared understanding of where to focus your efforts.** At this point, you may have generated a list with several opportunities for improvement and innovation—likely too many to do well. Remember, it's always better to do a few things well than many things poorly. To narrow down your list to a more manageable set of activities, we recommend you put your list of proposed improvements on a wall chart. Give each person on your leadership team three dots or stars and let them vote on what they believe ought to be your improvement priorities for the following semester or year.

4. **Now, develop a big goal.** By this point, you should be getting clear about where to focus your efforts, yet it's important to discuss one more critical question: As you look across the improvement pathways, what is most important for you, *right now*? And by right now, we mean within a defined time period—likely a semester or school year. This question will force you to focus on just one thing—a "rallying cry" for your school—the *one focus* that's most critical for your school in *the current school year*. Ask yourselves this question: Which What Matters Most component, if improved, would enable us to move closer to our vision and result in our viewing the year as a success? Conversely, what's the *one thing* that if we don't get done (or we do wrong) might undercut everything else we might get right? This *one focus* should become your big goal, the subject of your undivided attention. That doesn't mean you won't bother with anything else. You may delegate some things to particular school staff or see some activities as subordinate to others (for example, encouraging a more collaborative culture in order to improve teaching practices) so long as it doesn't divert energy, resources, or attention away from the one big thing you absolutely, positively must accomplish in the next 90–180 days.

Transfer information from this tool to the ToolTracker on page 106. Now, you will begin to align your focus with your vision.

Telling Your Story

You've accomplished a lot in this phase! So far, you have:

- Reviewed data and created an urgency and more specificity around your vision.

- Identified bright spots, both by expanding on your data to recognize positives to accompany the not-so-positives, and by conducting instructional rounds to observe bright spots in action.

- Placed your school along the continuum of improvement for each of the five What Matters Most components.

- Narrowed your focus to what matters most, right now.

All of this work supports your school's improvement and innovation journey, helping develop a narrative that says: Where we are is unacceptable because it's incompatible with our moral purpose; therefore, we must do things differently, and when we do, things will be better.

At this point, it's important to bring all your ideas together in a simple narrative that helps tell the story of where your school is and where you're headed. This narrative conveys a sense of urgency and provides clear connections to teaching, learning, student success, and engagement. It also offers a motivating image of the brighter future your entire school community will create together.

Use Tool #9 on the next page to guide you in crafting a narrative about your school. What do you want to say about where you're headed?

Tool #9: Telling your story

This tool is designed to help you develop a compelling narrative for your improvement/innovation effort, simply by filling in the blanks below.

1. Using the data and ideas you collected in the previous tools, follow the prompts below to craft a brief story describing your vision for teaching and learning in your school.

Our data show that _____

_____

That's unacceptable to us because, deep down, we believe _____

_____

_____

Therefore, we must ensure that our teaching is _____

and that learning is _____

for all students.

We must act now because _____

_____

_____

When we do this, we'll create a school where _____

_____

_____

2. Having trouble drafting a cohesive narrative? Allow each member of the team three minutes to craft and share a compelling 60-second narrative based on your school's story.

3. Listen to each presentation, noting the similarities and differences in the narratives.

4. Now, work together to identify common themes and pertinent ideas. Use these to hone your compelling narrative into one that you can share with others, who in turn could convincingly share the narrative with even more people. This, after all, is the real power of stories—they're memorable, repeatable, and capture the truth of our experiences.

With your story completed, turn to the ToolTracker on page 107 to record it there.

Phase 2 is a significant undertaking as it uses a variety of data to establish your course for action. In the next chapter, you'll identify the specific strategies for improvement that you want to use to achieve your goals.

Phase 3: Focus on Teaching and Learning

How will we help people transform professional practice?

Focusing on What Matters Most

By mapping themselves onto the improvement and innovation pathways, Stillbrook K–8 School's RIT saw they'd made significant progress in many areas. They had, for example, articulated a curriculum and teachers had committed to following it; they had adopted a common approach to instruction; and students felt safe and respected.

"You know, doing this makes me feel better," Tom remarked. "We've come a long way. When we know *what* to do, we usually get it done."

"We've had a good leader, too," Belinda added, giving Janice a friendly wink.

"Thanks, but I now see where we can do better," Janice replied. "Starting with building a more collaborative school culture."

"So, is that where we should focus? School culture?" Belinda asked.

The group was silent for a moment until Oscar spoke. "Yes and no, I think. Yes, we need a more collaborative culture, but that can't be our *only* focus. We must work on the *work*, too—the stuff in the middle of the What Matters Most framework: curriculum and instruction."

"I agree," said Tom. "I've got a little hamster wheel spinning in my head about something."

"What's that?" asked Belinda.

"I wonder if where we put ourselves on these pathways might shed light on the data point that's giving us the most heartburn right now: low writing scores for our 7th and 8th graders."

"Hmm," Belinda replied, pensively chewing on the end of her pen. "So, we said that one of our bright spots is our curriculum alignment; we've got all students writing in earlier grades."

"And our data shows our students have pretty well mastered grammar and composition structure," Oscar interjected. "Yet when they go on to middle school, they seem to lack the ability to develop or support strong ideas. Why?"

"They haven't learned to *think*," Belinda observed, before adding, "I mean, *we* haven't *taught* them to think."

Everyone nodded in agreement. "Why is that?" Janice asked.

Belinda shrugged. "I could speculate lots of answers, but that's all I'd be doing: speculating. Maybe we should ask our teachers."

"Good idea," said Janice.

That week, Belinda and Tom combined their teacher teams for an expanded conversation, during which most people agreed that students needed to develop better critical thinking skills. So, why wasn't that happening? Belinda asked.

After a thoughtful conversation aided by an examination of some teacher "theories of action" linked to student curiosity, they arrived at an answer: We're not providing students with challenging learning tasks—tasks that engage them cognitively, asking them to analyze, evaluate, synthesize, and create.

A lively conversation followed when one teacher commented, "I totally agree with all of this—that we should be challenging our students to think. Yet it seems like what I'm giving my students is already too hard for them . . . at least a lot of them can't complete the work."

"Can't . . . or don't want to?" asked another teacher.

"That's a good question," replied the first teacher. "Maybe they're bored, or don't see the purpose of what I'm asking them to do."

"So, maybe there's a difference between *hard* and *challenging*," said yet another teacher.

That comment served as a pivotal moment. As a group, the teachers decided to focus on creating challenging learning tasks—tasks that were meaningful and engaging, yet cognitively demanding and guided by big ideas, while scaffolded to students' learning needs. And so it was that Stillbrook's "big goal" for professional learning emerged *from the inside out*: They'd spend the year developing and exposing students to challenging learning tasks.

A productive tension, however, soon emerged among the group; some were eager to rush out and try new ideas in their classrooms while others wanted to know, in clear and concrete terms, what was expected of them. In his usual reflective way, Oscar suggested a workable solution: Teachers would work together in smaller, grade-band teams to develop and study the creation of challenging learning tasks and then share out to the larger group what they were doing and learning. "We should develop new practices . . . but together," he said to nodding heads.

A few days later, though, as Janice sat in her office after school, she heard a soft knock.

She looked up to see Denise Gray standing in the doorway. Denise was the school's most veteran teacher—a veritable institution, having taught two generations of students. She was well-loved by many parents and known for her no-nonsense benevolence, stern one moment, yet caring the next. She could also be a thorn in the side of school administrators, especially when something didn't make sense to her.

When Janice had first assumed the role of principal, she and Denise came to loggerheads over a district-wide technology integration effort. Denise had produced reams of journal articles that questioned the value of technology in student learning. Eventually, Janice relented and let Denise sidestep technology in her lesson plans, perhaps because she half agreed with her. Denise seemed to return the favor a year later by becoming an outspoken champion of Janice's effort to get everyone to adopt a teaching model. After that, an uneasy alliance, or perhaps relationship of mutual respect, had formed between Janice and Denise.

After chatting about kids and grandchildren for a few minutes, Denise revealed the real purpose of stopping by the principal's office when she asked, "Are you OK with all of this?"

"All of what?"

"All of this talk about 'big ideas' and 'challenging tasks.' It seems contrary to the teaching model we've adopted. Getting kids to be curious is nice, but I need to make sure my kiddos know their math facts, their spelling words and vocabulary terms, and the difference between a noun and verb. If they don't get those things, they're sunk."

Janice asked Denise why she thought focusing on learning tasks would detract from helping students master the basics. Denise replied that she thought it was unnecessary to "get too fancy" in the classroom. Besides, what she was doing was working, so, "If it isn't broken, why fix it?"

An image of Denise's immaculate classroom flashed into Janice's mind; she had a place for everything, and everything in its place. Janice realized what she was asking Denise to do was "messy" and told Denise as much, adding that the emphasis on challenging learning tasks wasn't intended to *replace* the teaching model, but build on it.

"I had some of these same concerns myself," Janice acknowledged. "But I've come to think of it this way: Our teaching model is like learning to play four chords on the guitar. You can play a lot of songs with them, but after a while, the songs get stale. This is what our kids are experiencing. We need to add a few more chords to our repertoire and get better at integrating everything in a way that builds on our fundamentals so that it's more engaging for students. Does that make sense?"

Denise allowed that it did and thanked Janice for her time. They parted amicably, but afterward, Janice felt a pit in her stomach; she could tell Denise wasn't on board. And if Denise wasn't on board, her gravitational pull on other teachers could bring the whole effort crashing to the ground. ∎

Keep the Focus on Teaching and Learning

At last! You're ready to determine *how* your school will approach your selected area of focus—what matters most to you, right now.

Remember, to improve learning outcomes, your efforts should focus on the core of What Matters Most: curriculum and instruction. Addressing school culture is important because it improves the "core business" of schooling: teaching and learning. Similarly, providing whole-child student supports is crucial, yet remains exactly that: a *support* for learning. If curriculum is misaligned or poorly implemented, or teaching is weak and inconsistent, student learning will suffer.

If you haven't already, one of the most important things you can do in your school, in fact, is adopt a consistent *model* for instruction, which is different than a *framework*.

What's the Difference?

Frameworks seek to arrange complex information into manageable categories. For the past decade or more, school systems nationwide have adopted evaluation frameworks that attempt to capture the complexity of teaching into a handful of categories, which themselves comprise dozens of smaller elements. Such frameworks presume to say, "Here are all of the things we know that good teachers do, so you should do these things, too—with increasing levels of consistency and intensity."

In many ways, teaching frameworks attempt to put in one place everything that great teachers do. And that's certainly helpful. However, most frameworks fail to provide a clear process that teachers can follow and emulate in their classrooms to support better student learning—a *model* for instruction (or, better yet, for *learning*). We might think of it this way: While a framework says, "Try to incorporate all of these things into your teaching," a model says, "Do these things in this sequence to guide student learning."

Decades of research on talent development shows that a critical, early phase of developing expertise includes modeling others' practices. Novice artists copy masters. Amateur athletes watch videos of professionals. Garage bands cover other people's songs. Similarly, teachers—especially those in the process of forming their professional practice—benefit from having a model of instruction to follow.

A Model for Practice

We offer our own version of such a model in Figure 6, which integrates cognitive science on how people's brains develop deep knowledge and skills with McREL's research on effective classroom instructional strategies, as reported in *Classroom Instruction That Works,* 2nd Edition (Dean, Hubbell, Pitler, & Stone, 2012). You'll notice that we've framed each stage in the process in terms of student *learning*—what happens in students' brains as they learn. This is quite intentional as it's where the action really occurs in a classroom. Also, it's easier for teachers to make the shift to more personalized learning strategies when they focus on *learning* instead of just *instruction*.

Figure 6. A model for teaching and learning

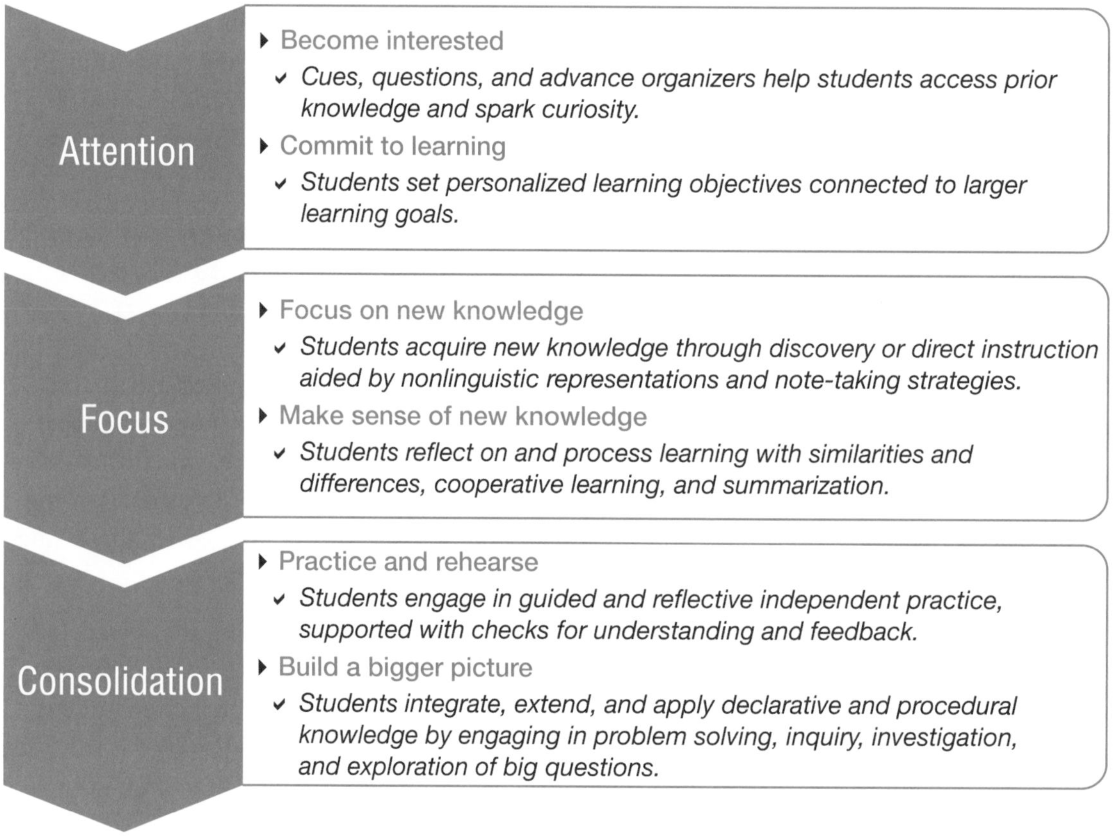

Attention

▸ Become interested
✔ *Cues, questions, and advance organizers help students access prior knowledge and spark curiosity.*
▸ Commit to learning
✔ *Students set personalized learning objectives connected to larger learning goals.*

Focus

▸ Focus on new knowledge
✔ *Students acquire new knowledge through discovery or direct instruction aided by nonlinguistic representations and note-taking strategies.*
▸ Make sense of new knowledge
✔ *Students reflect on and process learning with similarities and differences, cooperative learning, and summarization.*

Consolidation

▸ Practice and rehearse
✔ *Students engage in guided and reflective independent practice, supported with checks for understanding and feedback.*
▸ Build a bigger picture
✔ *Students integrate, extend, and apply declarative and procedural knowledge by engaging in problem solving, inquiry, investigation, and exploration of big questions.*

Developing Teacher Expertise

Mastering a learning model like this one is one of the most powerful techniques educators can use to improve student achievement. As we reported in *Simply Better: Doing What Matters Most to Change the Odds for Student Success* (Goodwin, 2011), multiple studies have shown that consistent adoption of a teaching model (like Explicit Direct Instruction) has a significant impact on student learning. Yet it is by no means the final step on the journey to innovation—at least not if we want to create personalized learning environments where students become curious and passionate about their learning. However, it's often at this point—feeling competent and comfortable with what we're doing—that many people stop improving. That's because going beyond this point requires what psychologist Anders Ericsson calls "conscious incompetence"—effortful concentration and, often, falling flat on our faces.

The biggest difference between champion and non-champion ice-skaters is that champions engage in *deliberate* practice—devoting most of their practice time to spins and jumps they haven't yet perfected. Non-champions, meanwhile, spend their practice time rehearsing moves they've already mastered. Engaging in deliberate practice is how experts not only expand their repertoire, but also develop multiple schema that allow them to size up problems and craft solutions from an extensive array of strategies (Newell & Simon, 1972). Simply stated, experts have in their mental toolbox a large collection of if-then statements: If X happens, then I do Y. This is the skill that allows a veteran quarterback to size up the defense and instantly call a better play.

Through deliberate practice, experts begin to integrate smaller steps into longer scripts—that's how chess grandmasters can think as many as eight moves ahead. These scripts also help experts look beyond their own actions and respond to what others are doing. For example, the biggest compliment one can pay a jazz musician is that she has "big ears"—the ability to play her own instrument while listening to fellow musicians and embellish on their riff during her own solo.

What Experts Do: Teacher Theories of Action

All of this is what educators in northern Melbourne observed when they toured the classrooms of expert teachers with highly engaged and curious students. Certainly, their practices reflected foundational elements of good teaching (e.g., using tried-and-true techniques such as learning objectives, questions, and cooperative groups), but it was how they integrated these techniques in their classrooms with intention that set them apart—and engaged their students. Hopkins and his colleagues (2015) distilled these expert behaviors into the following "teacher theories of action:"

- **Harness learning intentions, narrative, and pace.** Help students set and chart their own progress toward learning goals while keeping lessons lively, fast-paced, and linked together into a larger unit narrative with a clear sense of forward momentum.

- **Set challenging learning tasks**. Dial in the proper level of challenge for each student while offering them meaningful choices and cognitive challenges, and ensuring they master subject-specific vocabulary while exploring big ideas.

- **Frame higher order questions.** Master the ability to ask questions that prompt students to apply, analyze, evaluate, and synthesize information, while bundling it with other techniques, including "wait time."

- **Connect feedback to data**. Effectively dissect data about student progress to provide students with timely, non-evaluative feedback that encourages a growth mindset, reflective learning, positive self-talk, and ownership of learning.

- **Commit to assessment for learning.** Frequently check for understanding and use data from informal and formal assessments to guide changes to instruction.

- **Implement cooperative groups.** Create cooperative learning environments and experiences that require students to employ sophisticated levels of thinking and positive interdependence to solve big problems together.

These theories of action are examples of ways that experts build on the foundational elements of the learning model without departing from it—just as expert musicians build on their knowledge of chords and scales to write and perform creative music. As teachers become more expert in these theories of action, they seamlessly integrate the foundational elements of the learning model—for example, creating challenging learning tasks that capture student attention, helping them focus on new knowledge and consolidate it into long-term memory. It's also worth noting that at the core of each theory of action is the assumption that learning grows more powerful (and students grow more curious) when classrooms are no longer teacher-directed and student-experienced, but rather, student-owned and teacher-guided.

Balancing Intervention, Autonomy, and Support for Professional Practice

In the previous phase, you assessed your school's placement on the improvement and innovation pathways, and you identified the What Matters Most component on which you'll focus your energies. The next step is to determine the actions you'll take—the actual changes you'll make to teaching and learning—that will help your school move through the stages of improvement. Before you select actions, however, take a moment to think about what your school's placement along the pathways means for how you'll approach other aspects of your school, including your organizational culture and approach to leadership.

As shown in Table 3, if you're focused on "adopt better routines," you'll need to ensure your school culture understands and values the need for clarity, cohesion, and consistency. On the other hand, if you're ready to "develop collegial expertise," you'll likely need to focus on developing opportunities and readiness for peer collaboration and coaching. Meanwhile, if you're working to "foster shared innovation," you may need to focus on creating a fail-forward culture that supports rapid-cycle innovation. As an RIT, you may also need to pivot your leadership style as you move along these improvement stages—from more directive leadership when adopting routines and ensuring consistency, to a more empowering style when developing expertise or fostering shared innovation.

Table 3. Aligning focus, leadership, and school culture with improvement stages

	Adopt better routines	Ensure greater consistency	Develop collegial expertise	Foster shared innovation
Improvement focus	Articulate curriculum and select teaching model	Ensure consistency in curriculum and instruction	Develop teaching expertise and adapt adopted curriculum	Foster teaching and curriculum innovations
Leadership behaviors	Set expectations and direct routines	Monitor and scaffold consistency	Support peer learning and coaching	Empower experimentation
School culture	Embrace routines	Commit to consistency	Create precision without prescription	Adopt fail-forward ethos

As a team, reflect on where you see your school on the pathway for your selected What Matters Most component. What kind of support—or what degree of autonomy—is appropriate for your school relative to this component?

The next tool will help you align your improvement efforts, allowing you to see that any changes you're making to your culture or organizational procedures ought to support and align with your core focus on teaching and learning. Remember, it's important to solicit input from the rest of the staff, to check that the perceptions of the RIT are shared, and to uncover any additional perspectives.

When teachers have the opportunity to give feedback, it helps with the change process. Thus, you should seek occasions to share your thinking with staff, soliciting their feedback on areas of ambiguity, eliciting their concerns, and modeling your own inquiry and curiosity as a team in striving for your vision.

Tool #10: Connecting vision with action

This tool uses the stages of improvement to create a simple snapshot for your school, clarify your teaching and learning focus, and then connect that focus back to your vision and moral purpose.

Your vision: _____

_____

Check the boxes that reflect your current bright spots that are complete or nearly always true. Unchecked boxes will point toward opportunities for growth.

	Adopt better routines	Ensure greater consistency	Develop collegial expertise	Foster shared innovation
Curricular pathways to success	☐ We have aligned and developed our curriculum.	☐ Our curriculum is consistently enacted.	☐ We collaborate to adapt our adopted curriculum.	☐ Feedback from teachers and students guides curriculum adaptation.
Challenging, engaging, and intentional instruction	☐ We have identified and adopted a teaching model.	☐ We consistently use our teaching model.	☐ We collaborate to create precision without prescription.	☐ We elicit student voice in our instructional design.

Pause at the first unchecked boxes (reading left to right). Likely, this points to what matters most now, shown below.

What matters most *right now*	We must align, articulate (e.g., with pacing guides), and monitor use of curriculum. **and/or** We must identify and monitor adoption of a teaching/learning model.	We must provide models and materials to ensure consistency. **and/or** We must coach and build skills to implement the model more consistently.	We must adapt the curriculum we've adopted to challenge and engage students more effectively. **and/or** We must build from the model to grow teacher expertise (e.g., teacher theories of action).	We must create competencies and systems to empower self-paced, personalized learning. **and/or** We must build on teaching expertise to create next practices that empower student learning.
Key question	What curriculum/ instructional model will we implement?	What part(s) of the curriculum/ instructional model must be more consistent?	What deep learning approach/expert teaching practice (e.g., theory of action) must we develop with precision?	What learning problem will we solve? What new approach to learning will we develop and test in a rapid cycle?

Now consider which other What Matters Most elements are already in place and which ones must be improved to support your teaching and learning focus. Check the boxes that reflect your current state.

Whole-child student supports	☐ We have behavior expectations and identify struggling learners.	☐ We have a safe school and target support for learners.	☐ We have resilient students and expert learning support in classrooms.	☐ Our students are safe, persistent, passionate, and well-supported learners.
High-performance school cultures	☐ We have vision, values, and routines for continuous improvement.	☐ We embrace and adhere to shared values and procedures.	☐ We collaborate and coach one another to improve our performance.	☐ We are comfortable failing forward, finding and solving problems together.
Data-driven, high-reliability systems	☐ We regularly collect data about our school.	☐ We have common data protocols to guide our database.	☐ We use common assessment data to guide learning.	☐ We study and scale up teacher innovations and next practices.

Describe your current bright spots upon which you will build.	
Describe how your actions will move you closer to your vision.	
Describe how your actions will help fulfill your moral purpose.	

Based on your assessment, is the selected approach the right one to enable you to move toward your vision? If not, you may need to revisit this process. Use the ToolTracker on page 108 to help you bring together your ideas about vision, action, and leadership.

Imagine you have a friend whose restaurant is failing. She's in danger of losing her life's savings and abandoning her lifelong dream to own her restaurant and asks you for advice. What should she do?

Consider for a moment what questions you might ask her. You might wonder if her prices are too high or if her restaurant is in a good location. You might look around the restaurant itself to see if it has a nice ambience and friendly staff. Ultimately, though, you'd want to try the food. After all, people will drive out of their way, pay a few extra bucks, tolerate so-so customer service, and eat in a place with lackluster décor if the food is consistently good. Likely, you'd advise your friend that if she loads up her menu with great-tasting dishes—and makes sure they taste great every day of the week—everything else will follow. After all, *food* is the core business of restaurants.

A similar idea applies to schools: Get curriculum and instruction right and success is soon to follow. Sure, we must attend to other conditions, including providing student supports, developing a school culture, and creating systems to ensure data-driven high reliability. But remember, those conditions are usually subordinate to ensuring that every day, students have opportunities to learn challenging content with good instruction. *That* is the "core business" of schooling.

As obvious as this sounds, we often encounter school leaders who focus their school improvement efforts on changing other things—whether it's sprucing up the school newsletter, enforcing student (and faculty) dress codes, or revamping the school playground. Such changes are often easier to make because they usually don't disrupt anyone's deeply held beliefs and routines. At most, they may ask them to change an easy habit, like putting on nicer clothes in the morning.

Ultimately, focusing on teaching and learning means asking people to change ingrained behaviors, which is never easy for anyone. Yet any change worth making—any change that is likely to *change student learning outcomes* and create joyful, curious learning in your school—will likely require everyone in the school to change in some significant way.

So, now that you know *what* you want people to do, the next three phases of this guidebook will help you understand how and *why* people change their behavior, so that you and your school community can rally around and support each other through change—which, as we'll see, is a key, and often overlooked, secret to change.

Phase 4: Support Professional Learning and Collaboration

How do we change together?

Learning to Let Go: Making the Pivot to Inside-Out

Over the weekend, to clear her mind, Janice went to the local rec center and rejoined a Zumba class that she'd skipped for several months while tied up at work. Soon, she found herself enraptured by the music, her instructor's inspirational quips ("Sweat is your fat crying!"), and the other class members' whoops of encouragement. The hour passed quickly. Afterward, she felt exhausted—but strangely renewed. "I should do this more often," she thought.

On her way home, she reflected on how much harder she exercised in the class than when she was at home alone with an exercise DVD. Suddenly, she had an epiphany she couldn't wait to share with her RIT on Monday.

Two days later, Belinda stopped Janice a few seconds into her story. "Wait . . . you do Zumba?" Belinda asked, struggling to picture her straight-laced principal doing something so free-spirited.

"Yeah, I love the music," Janice replied. "And shaking my groove thing," she added with a wry grin that made everyone laugh.

"But what struck me was that no one was forcing me to work out as hard as I was," Janice continued. "My instructor didn't have any positional authority over me, yet she brought out the best in me—partly because she was working harder than anyone in the room. My classmates, too, made me work harder—not because we were competing, but because I shared their enthusiasm. I also learned from them, seeing how they do the moves, so I could do them better.

"I found myself thinking that's the essence of a collaborative culture. And maybe what's been missing for us. What lies ahead of us is a different kind of challenge. There's no new program we can adopt or simple fixes we can make. We must learn together—as professionals."

Oscar smiled. "I'm glad to hear you say that. I think our teachers are 'PD'd' out. They'll probably run the other way if we send them to the gym for another 'spray-and-pray' professional development session or tell them to implement yet another new program. I think that could be why our close reading and mathematics argumentation stuff didn't go so well last year."

Tom nodded. "I agree. The trainers we brought in were good, but a lot of people felt like it was coming out of left field—like it wasn't really the problem they wanted to be solving."

"I think we're pretty unique here, too, as a K–8 school with a diverse student body," added Belinda. "Well, I'm sure every school thinks they're unique, but that's why bringing things in from the outside tends to be met with resistance. This whole effort we're doing right now is so important, so potentially transformative for us, that it has to feel like your Zumba class, Janice—where we're learning from and encouraging each other to create awesome, curiosity-filled learning experiences for kids."

"I like that image," Tom added. "Belinda and I can be the aerobics instructors, encouraging people to push themselves to do more than they thought possible for themselves and their kids. If we see someone who needs some extra help, we'll spend some extra time with them, giving them pointers. Meanwhile, we'll help everybody make *each other* better. It's like two-dimensional coaching—leader-to-follower and peer-to-peer."

Oscar nodded. "And as long as we tie it all back to shared frameworks and rubrics, we'll keep moving in the same direction— like a Zumba class, not a dance party with everyone randomly dancing to music on their own headphones. As for me, now that I know my boss's musical tastes"—he shot Janice a mischievous wink—"I can't wait to go back to my office and start blasting salsa music." ∎

Turning the "Big Goal" Into Action: Job-Embedded Professional Learning and Coaching

Congratulations! Your team has selected an area of focus and a "big goal" for change. Now it's time to dig into the work of improvement and innovation *at the classroom level*. A focus on improvement at the classroom level, where teachers can have the greatest impact on student learning, is one of the characteristics that sets a Curiosity Works approach to school improvement apart from many other approaches.

As an RIT, your next task is to determine how to cultivate curiosity and engage teachers in professional learning to achieve the desired outcomes for your school. What supports (e.g., professional learning, coaching, modeling, etc.) will teachers need to adopt new routines with consistency, develop expertise, or create innovations?

As Bruce Joyce and Beverly Showers reported in 2002, most forms of professional development do little to help teachers transfer knowledge into action. In fact, only when teachers have opportunities to learn the *theory* behind a teaching strategy, observe the *strategy* being demonstrated, *practice* using the new technique in their own classrooms, and receive *feedback* and *coaching* for professional learning do we typically see shifts in their practice. This progression of professional learning is illustrated in Figure 7 on the following page.

For change to occur, everyone involved must develop a deep understanding of both the change initiative itself and the plan of action. And at the heart of any change is true professional learning, which is most effective when we shift from an event-oriented approach to staff development (e.g., attending a workshop) to ongoing professional learning that is embedded in the work of the school.

In addition, the improvement stage where you placed your school on the pathways will guide how you balance the need for more directive intervention versus greater teacher empowerment and autonomy. Schools with practices situated primarily in the "adopt better routines" range likely require a focus on foundational supports to create a consistent,

Figure 7. Progression of professional learning

Theory	Demonstrate	Practice	Feedback	Coaching
Explain and justify the new approach to practice.	Model the new practice by demonstrating how to implement it.	Teachers introduce the new practice in their classrooms.	Teachers receive feedback about their use of the new practice from their professional learning team.	Teachers receive individualized coaching that helps them improve their use of the new practice.

supportive environment for teaching and learning. Schools with practices in the "develop collegial expertise" range may need to focus on embedding practices deeply across the school, and then stretch themselves to collaboratively refine their practices and press for even greater outcomes for students.

Peer observation can be the best way to develop professional practices that have a predictable impact on student achievement. This form of professional learning capitalizes on teachers' expertise and is implemented via small, high-functioning teams, often triads, that collaborate regularly.

One characteristic of high-achieving schools is that performance development and management are frequently based on teacher portfolios of practice (Hopkins & Craig, 2015). These portfolios draw on precise specifications of practice using protocols to guide implementation, peer observation, and coaching teams. This approach to performance development and management is a hallmark of securing change in teacher practice from the inside out. It is an approach that explicitly supports teachers to extend their repertoire of high-value teaching practices through collaborative exploration and feedback. They learn by doing and reflecting.

In contrast, "top-down" approaches impose teaching practices through hierarchical direction. While schools that are developing routines may benefit from some degree of top-down prescription as they initiate their improvement efforts, the intent is to move toward an approach that places responsibility for learning in the hands of teachers.

Keep in mind that an inside-out approach to professional learning doesn't mean that teacher teams simply select topics for professional learning based on their personal interests. This would result in a variety of disconnected activities occurring across the school. Rather, all professional learning activities are deeply and intentionally connected to the school improvement and innovation focus, with teacher teams working collaboratively to contextualize their learning to better meet the needs of their students.

So, how do you design effective professional learning? The following tool will help you design meaningful professional learning activities that lead to changed teacher practices, which in turn lead to enhanced student achievement.

Tool #11: Assess your professional learning needs

This tool will help you assess how well your school's current professional learning practices reflect the design principles of effective professional learning, as well as the degree of autonomy your teachers need to develop their professional expertise. Some of these ideas may be new to you or you may find your school hasn't enacted one or more of the principles. That's OK! The point of this tool is to assess openly and honestly the structures you have in place and view your gaps as opportunities to more effectively translate goals into professional learning and results.

As a team, review the checklist of Professional Learning Design Principles that follows. We offer it not as a lockstep, "read-do," but rather as a "do-confirm" list of the principles of effective professional learning. Through conversation, identify which of these you already have in place and practice consistently across your school.

Design Principle 1: We allocate space and time to teacher inquiry and professional learning.

At our school:

☐ We have a master schedule for time and locations of team meetings.

☐ We follow protocols so everyone knows our meeting procedures (e.g., whom to notify when a meeting is rescheduled, how to distribute meeting notes).

☐ We protect team meeting time from interruptions to the extent possible.

☐ Administrators partner with teams in addressing concerns about time and space, as needed.

Design Principle 2: Research and data guide teaching models and strategies.

At our school:

☐ All decisions about instructional models and strategies are informed by research.

☐ We choose instructional models and teaching strategies that are evidence-based.

☐ We use data to collaboratively refine our practices, evolving best practice into next practice.

Design Principle 3: We regularly study the impact of teaching models on student learning.

At our school:

☐ Teams collaboratively determine the formative assessment data that will be collected as we implement instructional models and strategies.

☐ Teams agree to and implement data collection plans.

☐ Teams collaboratively analyze and interpret data.

☐ Teams discuss what is revealed about student learning from the data and use that information to plan next steps.

☐ We highlight bright spots in data to identify areas that might support student growth and advance team professional practice even more.

Design Principle 4: We invest in expanding teachers' repertoires of effective practices.

At our school:

- ☐ We use a continuous improvement cycle process, for example, "study, do, reflect, and act."

- ☐ We follow protocols to support continuous improvement, for example, testing hypotheses about our teaching strategies/theories of action and their impact on student outcomes.

- ☐ We disaggregate data from our continuous improvement process to identify new patterns or anomalies and guide our theories of action.

- ☐ We identify and integrate successful practices into our teaching and, after studying both effectiveness and implementation data, revise or abandon practices that aren't getting results.

Design Principle 5: We align professional learning with school improvement plans.

At our school:

- ☐ Professional learning is explicitly linked to school goals.

- ☐ Teams align their focus of professional learning and inquiry with school goals.

- ☐ Teacher teams develop practice for a common model of teaching or theories of action.

- ☐ Professional learning helps teachers make the shift from teacher-owned and student-experienced learning environments, to learning that is student-owned and teacher-guided.

Design Principle 6: We share new insights and innovations across the school/system.

At our school:

- ☐ We have formal processes and structures for sharing team learning across teacher teams.

- ☐ We embrace our successes and our missteps as opportunities to learn and improve.

- ☐ We look for opportunities to learn about and share with teams from other schools in our district, region, and beyond.

1. Individually, identify three actions from the checklists that will elevate professional learning in your school. Increasing consistency in any of these practices counts as an action. If your school is in the *adopt better routines* or *ensure greater consistency* stage of improvement, you'll want to focus on consistency in your practices.

   _____

   _____

   _____

2. Using a separate piece of paper or flipchart, compile the actions identified by individuals into a single list.

3. Now, with your full list in front of you, come to consensus about the three actions you will take next to have the greatest impact on professional learning in your school.

Turn to page 109 and use the ToolTracker to list the three actions that your RIT determined will have the greatest impact on professional learning in your school.

Better Together: Supporting Peer Coaching

In the Curiosity Works approach to school improvement and innovation, peer coaching forms the basis for professional learning. Peer coaching supports curiosity and motivates teachers to strengthen their instructional practice by observing one another and offering "critical friend" feedback.

In a true peer coaching model, teachers work collaboratively to identify and address problems of practice in their own classrooms or focus on a collaboratively identified schoolwide problem of practice. Recalling our improvement and innovation stages, these teachers are developing collegial expertise and, if they engage with other teams, may also be fostering shared innovation.

Peer coaching can support every stage of improvement and innovation, yet may take on a slightly different character in each stage. Figure 8 illustrates this progression, describing key areas of focus for peer coaching across the continuum.

Figure 8: Peer coaching across the improvement and innovation stages

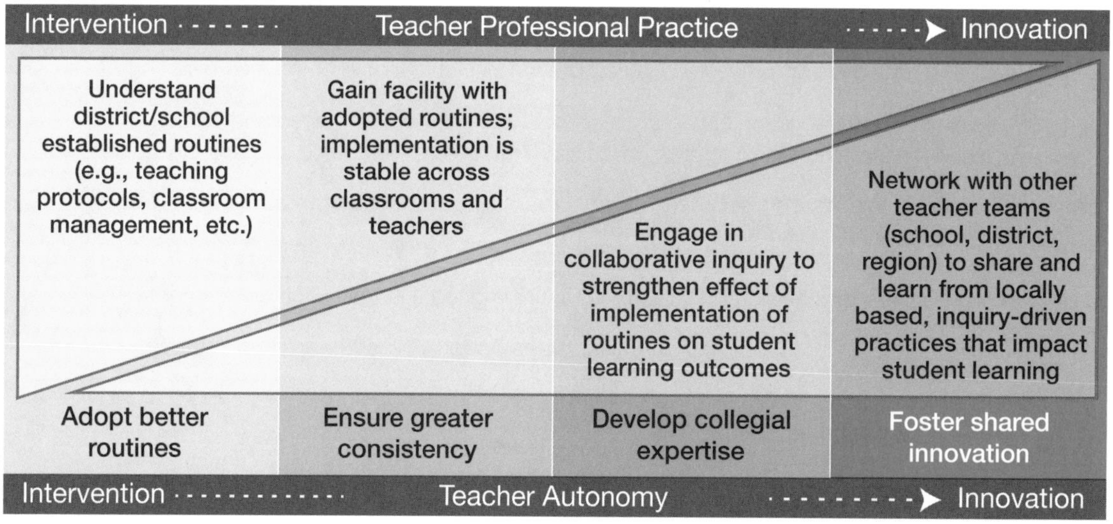

You might be wondering why we advocate for peer coaching as a foundation for professional learning, knowing that research has often found mixed results for teacher coaching. It's true, not all forms of teacher coaching are effective; thus, it's important to design peer coaching approaches that follow this advice from research (Goodwin, 2015):

- Coaching should support an agreed-upon, research-based *model* of teaching and learning. Without one, coaching feedback can become idiosyncratic or based on personal preference and do little to advance consistency or quality in teaching. Moreover, while many schools have *frameworks* for evaluating teachers, such frameworks often fail to illustrate what good teaching actually looks like in a classroom. This is what *models* for teaching and learning provide.

- Teachers tend to be too concerned with being nice when giving feedback to one another. Thus, coaching and feedback protocols are needed to encourage teachers to invite critical feedback from their peers and for teachers to deliver feedback to their colleagues. Non-evaluative peer coaching rubrics can also support peer coaching conversations as teachers work together to move toward higher levels of rubrics.

- Coaching can take two forms: *vertical* coaching (an expert giving feedback to a novice) and *lateral* coaching (peers providing feedback to one another). Schools can use both approaches simultaneously—for example, using more intensive vertical coaching to support novice or struggling teachers while employing lateral coaching to support all other teachers. Lateral coaching is less likely to be effective, at least initially, if the teachers' overall skills and knowledge are low.

Hopkins (2016) has defined six principles for peer coaching (Table 4).

Table 4. Principles for peer coaching

PRINCIPLES FOR PEER COACHING	
1	Peer coaching builds communities of teachers who continuously engage in the study of their craft.
2	Peer coaching partners increase their ability to teach students how to learn, and to analyze transactions between teacher and student.
3	Peer coaching provides a safe environment in which to learn and perfect new teaching models, experiment with variations of strategies, teach students new skills, and examine results. *(Peer coaching eliminates hierarchical power structures.)*
4	In peer coaching, teachers learn from one another as they plan teaching (instruction), develop support materials, watch one another work with students, and think about how their behavior influences students' learning.
5	The primary function of peer coaching partners is to learn by observing, and help colleagues by providing information about student responses. *(The purpose of peer coaching is not to give expert advice.)*
6	Peer coaching teams are committed to collecting data—they plan: • How they will monitor the implementation of new teaching and learning strategies. • How they will determine the impact of each strategy on their students.

Getting Started with Peer Coaching

Peer coaching, in its most basic form, involves teachers engaging in an observation-feedback cycle to learn from, and with, one another. Observations and feedback can be for one teacher to learn from another, for teachers to better understand what happens in their colleagues' classrooms, or for teachers to give one another feedback on their use of an instructional practice they have agreed is important. It's this last use of peer coaching that we encourage: teachers working together to study, implement, and give feedback to one another on a specific instructional practice for improving student learning.

While peer coaching can occur with two or more teachers, we advocate a triad model in which three teachers rotate among the roles of coach, coachee, and observer. Figure 9 below illustrates these three roles and their interactions. Key to the triad relationship is that all three teachers are involved in determining the focus for coaching and feedback. Often, especially for schools working to develop consistent routines, this focus is schoolwide.

Figure 9. Teacher peer coaching in a triad model

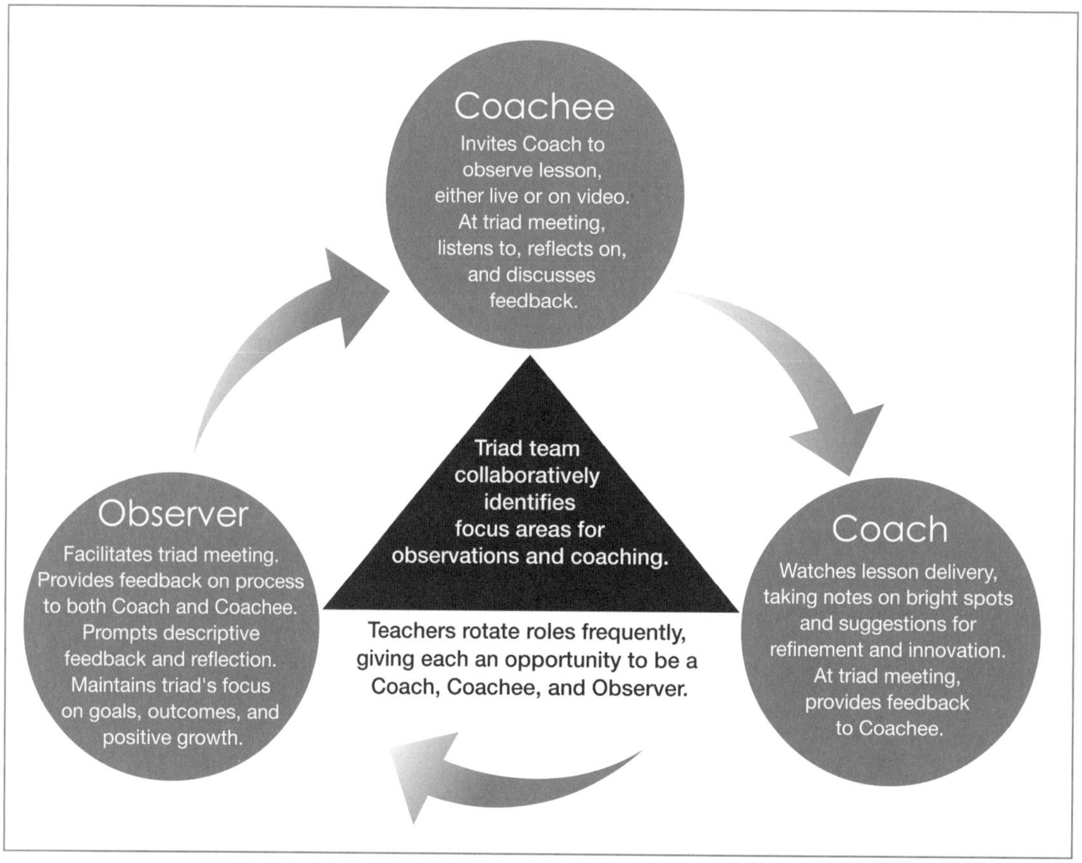

Coachee
Invites Coach to observe lesson, either live or on video. At triad meeting, listens to, reflects on, and discusses feedback.

Observer
Facilitates triad meeting. Provides feedback on process to both Coach and Coachee. Prompts descriptive feedback and reflection. Maintains triad's focus on goals, outcomes, and positive growth.

Coach
Watches lesson delivery, taking notes on bright spots and suggestions for refinement and innovation. At triad meeting, provides feedback to Coachee.

Triad team collaboratively identifies focus areas for observations and coaching.

Teachers rotate roles frequently, giving each an opportunity to be a Coach, Coachee, and Observer.

Once the triad is established, the coaching cycle is reminiscent of a study-do-reflect-act cycle of continuous improvement:

- Teachers plan together exactly how they will implement the strategy in their classrooms.
- The coachee volunteers to implement the plan, while the coach and observer observe.

- The team determines what they'll look for and the kind of feedback they'll provide to the coachee in a post-observation conference.

- The team decides if they need to make adjustments to their strategy implementation plan.

- Then, another teacher volunteers to be observed, and the cycle continues.

Figure 10. Continuous improvement cycle

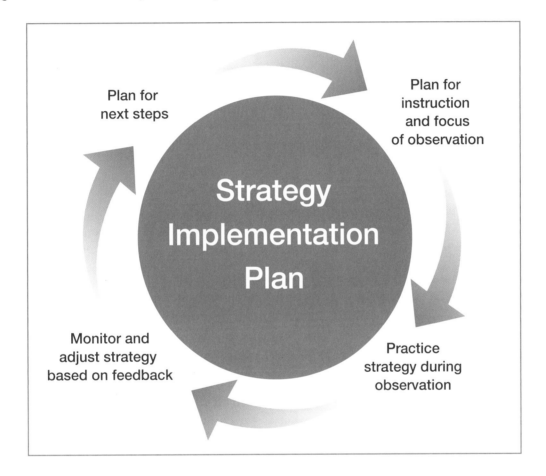

In this process, the focus of coaching, whether vertical or lateral, is your selected approach to improvement. For example, if the initial strategy selected is to adopt and consistently implement an instructional model, the peer coaching plan would involve teachers using the model to plan a lesson, one teacher teaching the lesson, and peers providing feedback about implementation of specific elements of the instructional model.

Rethinking Professional Learning

Ideas can be powerful. That's because how we *think* about something often influences what we *do*—even when those thoughts are subtle or even subconscious. Consider, for a moment, how leaders tend to think about professional learning. On the surface, many approaches look the same: We "give" teachers some professional learning, tell them to apply new practices in their classrooms, and dispatch instructional coaches to help them do it.

Yet, as James Spillane, a researcher at Northwestern University, found when he examined reform efforts in nine districts in Michigan, those surface similarities "camouflaged substantial differences in the underlying theories of teacher learning and change" (2000, p. 23)—differences that reflected what Spillane argued were *behaviorist, situated,* and *cognitive* views of change. Specifically, the vast majority (85%) of the 40 leaders studied by Spillane tended to cast professional development as a top-down strategy. For them, staff development consisted of transmitting information, usually from outside experts, to teachers and teacher coaches. They viewed professional development as a program of the central office, with which everyone needed to comply.

So, we understand that an inside-out approach to professional learning—one that expects most of the "action" to occur among teachers working together and often out of view of administrators—is likely to differ from common conceptions of how improvement "gets done."

Here's why this matters. We know from decades of research (see, for example, Pink, 2009) that a top-down (i.e., carrots-and-sticks) approach can motivate simple behaviors. But it will fall short when it comes to motivating more complex behaviors, like developing expertise or creating innovations. These tend to be motivated by intrinsic factors, including autonomy, mastery, and purpose—which are at the heart of an inside-out approach.

The point here is that if we don't occasionally examine our mental frames, we may act in ways that run counter to our intended purposes. And as we'll see in the next phase of this guidebook, nowhere is that more evident than in how we approach change—and those who resist change.

At this point, teachers in your school are ready to take responsibility for the work of school improvement. With a clear focus and a theory of action for improvement, teams—ideally, triad peer coaching teams—can own their learning. Together in their peer coaching teams, teachers can study, implement, refine, and continue practicing the selected strategy with students. The intent is for them to become increasingly precise, adapting the practice to meet the unique needs of their students. With continued practice, teachers will become more adept with the strategy and, over time, they should notice how use of the selected strategy is impacting students.

Phase 5: Embed Consistent, Deep Practice

How can we help others with the difficulties of change?

Leading One Person at a Time

By late October, peer coaching triads had taken root in Stillbrook K–8 School. Nearly every teacher was enthusiastically working with colleagues to create more challenging learning tasks in their classrooms. Janice and Oscar had re-worked teaching schedules so teams could plan lessons together, develop common assessments, and analyze data. Teams were using data and peer observations to identify bright spots—teaching practices that engaged students and left them bubbling with curiosity.

Using short surveys, they asked students how challenging they found their learning tasks to be and what teacher practices resonated with them. Teacher teams, in turn, began discussing student growth and engaging in shared planning, addressing not only the range of student needs, but their interests and how they aligned with the curriculum. Teacher talk also began to change from what *teachers* were *doing* in their classrooms to what their *students* were *discovering*. A new school culture was beginning to take hold and grow rapidly.

Yet there were some holdouts—a handful of teachers who were resisting the change despite Janice's pep talk. Some were openly derisive of the efforts in the faculty lounge. Others smiled and played along, nodding politely when they received feedback from their colleagues, but did little to change their practices.

Denise Gray's team complained to Oscar that Janice's nitpicking the tasks and assessments they were creating was holding them back.

Her heavy sighs and comments like "The kids are never going to get this" and "We should just focus on the basics," put a damper on meetings with her fellow 5th-grade teachers.

The pushback from Denise and the others troubled Janice. She saw it bordering on insubordination.

"So, what do we do about the holdouts?" she asked at the RIT meeting, which happened to fall on Halloween. "Do I need to put on a scary costume and go after them?"

The group chuckled. "Well, seeing as how we're not really doing costumes here anymore, that would probably bend the rules," Belinda said with a grin.

Janice smiled back, appreciating Belinda's attempt at levity. "Seriously, though, I don't like the nay-saying. I've seen how negative attitudes can spread like a cancer. I want to stop it. I know that as teacher coaches, you two should be good cops"—she gestured toward Tom and Belinda—"so do I need to play the bad cop? I'm happy to do that, you know."

The group nodded knowingly; Janice was definitely accomplished at lowering the boom on people. After a few seconds of awkward silence, Oscar spoke. "Let's give this whole inside-out thing a chance to work. I'm afraid if we try to force people into compliance, it will undermine what we're trying to do with intrinsically motivating teachers and students."

"I understand that, but what do we do about the folks who are dragging their heels?" Janice asked.

"Maybe we should figure out *why* they're not getting on board," Oscar offered. "I sense they may have their own individual reasons."

"I think that's true," Belinda added. "Some are probably just overwhelmed. They were barely keeping their heads above water before we moved in this direction, and now we're asking them to really deepen their practice. I think there may be a couple folks that haven't totally bought in yet. They're not really feeling it here"—Janice pointed to her heart—"and we may have a few old dogs who don't want to learn new tricks."

"Well, speaking as an old dog," Tom interjected with a smile, "I think we can bring them around, but we need to show them the old fashioned WIIFM—What's In It For Me."

"So, altogether, how many people are we talking about who aren't yet on board?" Janice asked.

"Five, maybe six," Belinda replied. "Out of 34, that's not bad."

"How many of that group are influencers—people who could sway others?" Janice asked again.

"Definitely a couple. Denise Gray comes to mind," Tom responded. "I think there's probably another five or six that are in wait-and-see mode. They're going along for now, but could backtrack if things don't go well."

"So, I'm right to be concerned about the holdouts?"

"Yes, absolutely," Tom replied.

"So, what we need to do is figure out *why* people aren't getting on board and then figure out what would bring them around," Janice said, appearing to come to a decision as she spoke.

"Let us help with that," Belinda said, indicating Tom and herself.

After the meeting, Oscar followed Janice into her office. He smiled as he sat down in a chair across from her desk.

"What are you smiling about?" Janice asked.

"Well, it's just my two cents, but I have a feeling we may look back on this whole interaction as sort of a turning point for us."

"How so?" Janice asked.

"Well, for starters, boss, what you did in there was difficult for you, I know. But it was really important. You stepped back a bit. And did you see what happened?"

Janice reflected for a moment. "Tom and Belinda stepped up."

"Exactly. And that's kind of new for us. So, let me ask you this: What can I do? How can *I* step up to help you?"

After pondering Oscar's question for a few seconds, Janice replied, "Help us learn more about change—why people resist it and what we can do to soften their resistance."

"Consider it done," Oscar replied.

A few days later, Janice had an epiphany that prompted her to stop by Denise Gray's classroom at the end of the day. After exchanging pleasantries, Janice asked how she was doing with all the changes.

"I'm still struggling a bit," Denise replied.

"Well, you know I wouldn't ask you to do anything I didn't think was right for kids."

Denise nodded.

"So, will you do me a favor, and just try *one* new strategy with your triad?"

"The green eggs and ham approach?" Denise said with a smile. "If I try it I might like it?"

"Exactly," Janice said, laughing. "See what happens and report back to me how it goes."

"OK," Denise said. "For you, Janice, I'll give it the old college try." ∎

Finding the Right Leadership Style: Directive vs. Empowering

Business researchers Ron Heifetz and Donald Laurie (1997) identified two key types of change in the life of any organization: *technical problems* and *adaptive challenges*. A technical problem, they reasoned, is one that can be solved with existing know-how and solutions. Essentially, with a technical problem, people know *what* to do and just need to do it. For leaders, solving technical problems is basically a management issue: They need to set expectations, provide timelines, and give marching orders. An adaptive challenge, on the other hand, requires solutions that lie outside of current know-how and modes of operating. Thus, addressing an adaptive challenge requires collaboration, creativity, experimentation, and also a very different style of leadership.

As schools move along the stages of improvement and innovation, they encounter both kinds of change, often needing to pivot between them. Early on, schools can make significant gains by addressing technical problems like enacting a curriculum in every classroom, establishing behavioral standards, and using a teaching model consistently. Eventually, though, they're likely to experience a performance plateau, and the way forward will become more ambiguous. For example, a school that makes great strides by enacting a curriculum in all classrooms may now find itself facing a thornier challenge—perhaps motivating students to engage in their own learning. Now the way forward will become less clear and likely only will be uncovered when teachers come together to identify new ways to ignite student curiosity and passion, perhaps, for example, through personalized learning.

Many who have studied systems reform efforts worldwide (Fullan, 2001; Hopkins & Craig, 2011; Barber & Mourshed, 2007) have observed this phenomenon on a large scale: When school systems rely only on technical solutions for improvement (e.g., standards, high-stakes testing, teacher qualifications), they get early gains which eventually taper off. Then they get stuck. They keep trying to apply what worked in the past—*technical solutions*—to what have become *adaptive challenges*.

Leaders get stuck, too. That's because different types of change require different leadership styles. When the problem is technical (e.g., implementing a new grading software), a *directive* approach is often more efficient and effective. For example, a study of health care teams implementing new routines found that teams with leaders who exhibited directive behaviors (e.g., assigning roles, giving clear directions, and setting expectations for compliance) were more successful than those with leaders who displayed *empowering* behaviors (e.g., sharing power, encouraging dissenting opinions, and promoting shared decision making). That's likely because, as the researchers concluded, "team reflection may be important for more complex tasks, such as innovative acts, but redundant for routine tasks" (Somech, 2006, p. 151).

A similar logic applies to schools: For quick gains, reflection and innovation are less important than simply applying better routines more effectively and consistently. Indeed, studies have found that teams led in a directive style initially outperform those led with an empowering style, yet their performance eventually peaks while teams led in an empowering style continue to improve, eclipsing teams led in a directive style. So, while empowering leadership behaviors may make teams less productive initially as they sort out how to work together, ultimately, by learning how to learn together, they can experience continued performance gains (Lorinkova, Pearsall, & Sims, 2013). The self-reflection tool on the next page will help you and your colleagues identify which leadership style—and related behaviors—are best suited to the challenges and opportunities your school faces now.

We've intentionally used the term *style* to describe these leadership behaviors. That's because they're changeable. Although some people gravitate more naturally toward one style than another, one approach or style is not necessarily always better than the other. Furthermore, both are learned behaviors. A person who's naturally more directive as a leader can learn to become more empowering, and vice versa. We might think of these differences as understanding when a leader needs to take a more assertive and fast-paced approach: when one needs to step "up" and direct the implementation of a technical solution versus when one needs to step "back," delegating decision making and allowing others to learn together and develop new solutions.

As with other decisions we have made in our journey thus far—identifying what matters most right now, where we should begin our journey, and how we can support professional learning through peer coaching—the stages of improvement and innovation can help inform the leadership style we should assume and our behaviors to support teaching and learning.

Take a look at Figure 11 below. You will notice that above and below the diagonal line we've included technical solutions and adaptive challenges, respectively. This suggests that, in general, as we move away from intervention and toward innovation we will encounter fewer changes requiring technical solutions and more that demand adaptive responses.

As leaders, we need to demonstrate a more facilitative and empowering style to foster a culture that is driven by the curiosity and inquiry necessary to spur innovation and move beyond the performance plateaus that tend to follow technical solutions. As such, we envision leadership behaviors shifting toward a more facilitative style as our improvement and innovation focus transitions from a need to ensure consistent implementation of routine practices to one that emphasizes developing collegial expertise, inquiry-driven learning, and the building of shared professional practice on what works for our students in our context.

Figure 11. Technical and adaptive challenges across the improvement and innovation stages

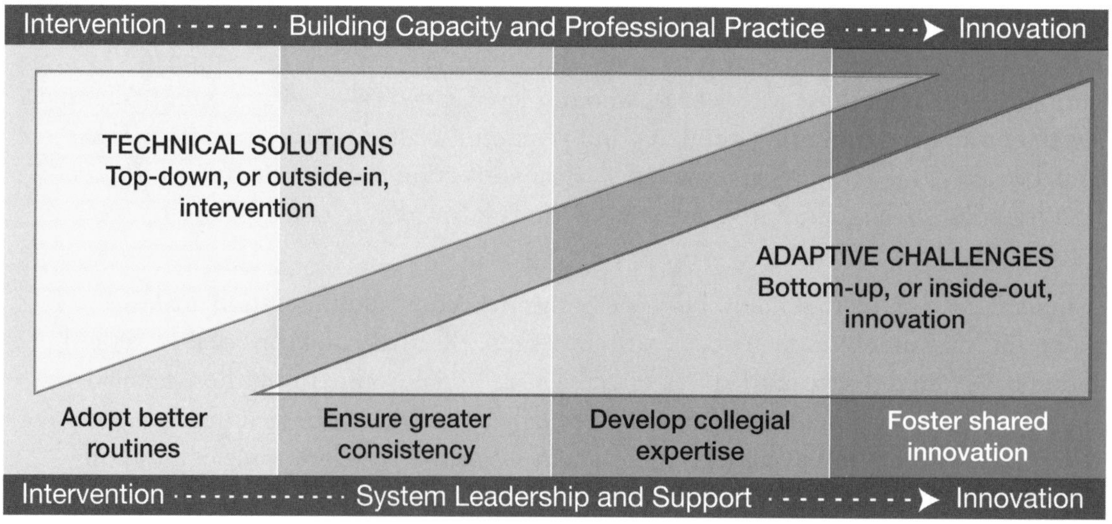

Tool #12: Directive versus empowering leadership styles

To help determine the leadership style your RIT should embody for your work, consider both your team's What Matters Most area of focus from Tool #8 (ToolTracker, pages 104-105) and the improvement stage most closely aligned with your school's current reality from Tool #7 (ToolTracker, page 106) as you respond to the following questions:

- Are the demands of this stage primarily associated with technical solutions or adaptive challenges? Why?

- Do we know what to do and just need to do it, or does the road ahead require a more complex approach?

Your answers should guide whether you adopt a more directive or empowering leadership style to support peer coaching teams as they work to strengthen their professional practice through collaborative learning and inquiry.

Turn to page 110 in the ToolTracker to record your responses before moving on.

Change Lies in the Eye of the Beholder

Now you have a high-level approach to distinguish directive from empowering leadership behaviors, and to see how they map onto technical solutions versus adaptive challenges. In the following sections, we'll help you carry out these behaviors in your school. We'll start by acknowledging that change is personal, and thus requires leaders to differentiate how they support individual responses to change.

Change is always personal. That's why the same change can be easy for one person yet difficult for another. For example, a straightforward technical solution, like adopting a new technology platform for reporting grades, may cause angst for teachers who don't understand the rationale for the change. Yet those same teachers might find an adaptive challenge, such as initiating inquiry-based learning, exhilarating and professionally rewarding—something they've been waiting their whole careers to do.

Thus, we must consider both the organizational context of a change (is it a technical problem or an adaptive challenge?) and the personal implications for those carrying out the change (see Figure 12 below). Will they embrace it as a straightforward next step, also known as a "first-order" change? Or will they perceive it as a "second-order" change, one that poses a significant challenge in their lives?

Figure 12. Resistance to change

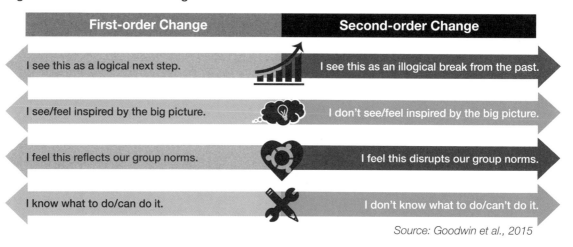

Source: Goodwin et al., 2015

In our research on school leadership (Goodwin et al., 2015), we found that when we experience change as second-order, we're more likely to view our leaders as being less effective in these four key areas:

- *Input* (supporting shared decision making)
- *Communication* (fostering open dialogue and accessibility to staff)
- *Culture* (promoting group cohesion and personal well-being)
- *Order* (providing and reinforcing clear routines and procedures)

Not surprisingly, these four areas map closely onto the reasons people may resist change:

- When we view change as an *illogical break from the past*, we want to offer **input** into the logic of decision making.

- When we believe a change *conflicts with our ideals*, we seek two-way **communication** and dialogue with our leaders to ensure we share their vision (and they share ours).

- If we feel change *conflicts with group norms*, we sense something amiss with **culture** and desire to restore well-being and group cohesion.

- If we fear we *lack the skills or knowledge* to do what's asked of us, we crave the clarity of re-established routines and **order**.

The need for a clear understanding of expectations when faced with change should be addressed early in the change process. William Bridges (2009) advocates the four "P's" that leaders and leadership teams must clearly communicate about a change initiative:

- **Purpose:** What are we trying to accomplish? Why do we believe this is the right approach for our school at this time?

- **Picture:** What will success look like? What benchmarks will allow us to know we're making progress?

- **Plan:** How will we do this? What are the details about how and when this change will occur?

- **Part:** What is the role of each member of the school community in the success of this initiative?

Purpose, as you might imagine, should be tightly connected to the moral purpose and vision that you described as part of the readiness actions you completed in Phase 1.

Communicating the *picture* of change is also connected to your vision. It includes identifying the indicators you will use to monitor progress and guide the supports you provide to move implementation forward. Some of these indicators may emerge from the data you reviewed in Phase 2, or from the tools that we have shared in previous phases or that will follow shortly. For example, the do-confirm list for Professional Learning Design Principle #2 (Tool #11 on page 62) can be used to determine not only your current state using evidence from research and practice, but also how consistent that use is among teams of teachers (the focus of this phase of our improvement and innovation journey). Once you know where you are on Design Principle #2, the do-confirm list can be used to guide identification of next steps for professional learning and coaching support, helping your teams make progress toward ideal implementation.

Details about the *plan* for your journey emerge as you describe what you have done to prepare for the work ahead, including ensuring readiness, and the phases of your inside-out approach to improvement and innovation. Grounding this communication in your values, purpose, and vision helps build and convey coherence in your approach, and also spurs the intrinsic motivation that will be needed to sustain progress when the road gets bumpy.

Bridges' final P, *part*, is clearly about the individual. Each person involved in a change needs to feel they have a role to play in pursuit of your vision, and to have clarity about what that role is and how it contributes to the vision. Implementation checklists can be helpful in communicating the nuts and bolts of a change effort, but may not clearly communicate *how* one is expected to implement it, and likely do not provide a scaffolded progression of skills that can be developed and strengthened over time. Tools that help with the *how* include performance rubrics and innovation configuration maps. Such tools describe key components of the change, and how those components might look when implemented weakly, adequately, and ideally. Self or team assessment using rubrics serve to clarify where our current set of practices lie on a continuum of skills and behaviors, and what we might work on next to advance our learning, professional practice, and effect on student outcomes.

Inspiring Change From the Inside Out

Pause a moment to reflect on your own experiences with change. Maybe you're thinking of the time your district adopted a new textbook or curriculum, or possibly the departure of your favorite boss and the arrival of your new one. Or maybe you're thinking of something more personal like the newly introduced formula in the shampoo you've been using for 20 years. Common to all of our responses to whatever change we experience, at least initially, is that they are almost always more emotional than intellectual. We must *feel* that we're competent, we belong in the group, we're involved in decision making, and we whole-heartedly embrace what we're doing.

That's not surprising. As Chip and Dan Heath (2010) note, our logical, conscious thoughts are really just tiny riders atop elephants of unconscious emotion. Our conscious brain likes to *think* it controls the elephant, and sometimes it does. But for the most part, the elephant pretty much goes where it wants to go. As a result, messages aimed at our "riders" often fail to move our "elephants." For example, when cardiac bypass patients who are told by surgeons they must change their lifestyle (i.e., change their diet, exercise more, quit smoking, reduce alcohol intake, and curb stress) or else they'll wind up back on the operating table (or worse, six feet under) only one in 10 are actually able to do so (Deutschman, 2006).

If *fear of death* isn't enough to motivate people to change their behavior, then fear of performing poorly at work probably isn't going to motivate us either.

Deutschman notes that the three F's of "fear, facts, and force" are usually insufficient to drive sustained changes in behavior. More effective are the three R's of "relate, repeat, and reframe" that appeal to our emotions and generate positive thinking. People are more likely to change when they can *relate* to the

Can a technical solution be inside-out?

How can our approach be inside-out if we need to adopt better routines with a more prescriptive approach? One of the distinguishing features of an inside-out approach to improvement is that the work is done by collaborative teacher teams, and is adapted to address needs as they arise. Even when solving a technical problem, teacher teams can still be at the core—the inside—of the learning and change process. For starters, they may have helped to identify the technical solution needed. They can also play a role in monitoring implementation of the effort and "owning" its success.

person asking them to change, have opportunities to *repeat* the change with support from others, and have the challenge *reframed* for them in a way that inspires new thinking and new hope. Thus, the cardiac patient might be encouraged to focus on what he's gaining (more energy, better physique, self-esteem, longer life) rather than on what he's giving up (smoking, drinking, relaxing).

Understanding the Emotional and Behavioral Sides of Change

When considering people's personal response to change we should also take into account their heightened concerns while adopting new practices and the actions and behaviors they apply to their work (Hall, Dirksen, & George, 2006).

Research supports the identification of seven distinct Stages of Concern that cluster into four major areas shown in Figure 13 (George, Hall, & Stiegelbauer, 2006; Hall & Hord, 1987). The ways we respond to these different concerns can help move implementation forward, or deepen the angst and stress that change can produce.

Figure 13. Major clusters of concern

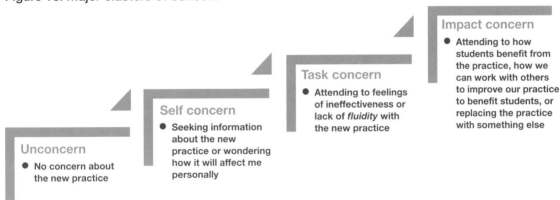

For instance, a teacher having difficulty completing all the expected components of reading instruction during a 90-minute block is likely to have *task concerns*. Providing the teacher with more information about the reading block components, checklists for tasks, or even encouragement that "it can be done" because you've seen it work, may only deepen the teacher's concern, potentially increasing her self-doubt and fear of negative consequences like poor evaluation or non-renewal of her contract. Actions that would support the teacher might include giving her some time to observe another teacher who's been more successful with the same tasks, or pairing her with a coach.

The key is to meet concerns head-on, and to provide the support necessary to ameliorate *self* and *task* concerns so that teachers are more focused on the impact of their teaching on students, both individually and collectively.

The next tool offers a protocol for understanding and responding to concerns.

Tool #13: One-legged interview to identify concerns

The one-legged interview (Hall & Hord, 2015), so named because the length of the conversation should be no longer than a typical person can stand on one leg, simply seeks to surface concerns another person is experiencing through questioning and expressions of genuine interest in their feelings. Here's a sample protocol to follow:

- Start with a simple question, like, "Hi, Frank, how is that work on prioritizing high expectations with your students going?"

- Frank's responses, and possibly one or two more questions, might lead you to find that Frank has been working with individual students to set their own expectations, but is worried they are setting them too high and may become discouraged if they aren't successful.

- Quickly size up Frank's responses along the four major clusters of concern from Figure 13 on page 77: unconcern, self, task, and impact.

- It's clear that Frank is expressing an *impact* concern—which is good news, because he's focusing on how the improvement initiative is affecting students.

With this knowledge about Frank's impact concerns, you might offer assurance that it's OK for students to experience struggles and setbacks, then share ideas about how to incorporate a lesson on the importance of failing forward into the focus on high expectations.

Another possible response may involve connecting Frank with a teacher who has been successful in facilitating individual student goal-setting. Or you might encourage him to share these concerns during an upcoming meeting with a peer coach. The key in responding to concerns is tailoring the support(s) to the individual concern expressed, to help move implementation and learning forward.

On page 111 of the ToolTracker, you'll find a worksheet with examples of hypothetical concerns. Work in pairs to determine the level of concern expressed in each. This will give you practice with the different levels before using the one-legged interview protocol with your teachers.

The ToolTracker also has space on page 112 to record your findings from the one-legged interviews.

Levels of Use

In addition to the emotional side of change that we all tend to undergo when our status quo is disrupted, the change process requires us to engage in and develop new behaviors that can, at least initially, feel uncomfortable and awkward.

As is often the case with our efforts at personal change—such as sticking to a diet, getting daily exercise, or quitting smoking—this is where our efforts to improve and innovate are likely to get derailed. It's much easier to stop doing something than it is to persevere and sustain effort despite discomfort and challenge. That's why it's important to not only monitor implementation, but also to provide support and encouragement, especially early in the change process.

Beyond gauging and supporting individual concerns, we can gain a sense of people's actions as they engage in the change process—how they are actually *using* the practice or practices that comprise the change or focus. Hall and colleagues (2006) have identified distinct ways that people use or don't use new practices. Although they describe three levels of non-use, we will assume that all staff are using (or are expected to be using) new practices. Through their research on implementation, Hall and Hord (1987) identified five ways in which individuals behave in response to change: mechanical, routine, refinement, integration, and renewal.

Figure 14. Behaviors of individuals regarding a specific change

Mechanical	Routine	Refinement	Integration	Renewal
Use may be awkward and fragmented. Adjustments are made to improve teachers' experience more than students'.	Use is "matter of fact" and stable with few or no changes being made.	Teachers begin to make adjustments with attention to how the changes impact students.	Teachers work with others to combine efforts to achieve a collective impact on students.	Teachers focus on making major changes in practice and/or identifying alternatives with even greater impact on students.

On the next page, you'll find a tool to guide the RIT in understanding levels of use and determining how to support deeper implementation.

Tool #14: One-legged interview to identify use

The one-legged interview, used earlier to better understand concerns, is also a useful tool when identifying levels of use. Sizing up people's use can be more difficult than identifying their concerns, largely because people tend to over-report their comfort in using a new practice out of a natural desire for others to see them as competent.

This short interview protocol and basic decision-making guide can help you elicit descriptions of how individuals are engaging in the change effort to determine their likely level of use. Similar to the actions you took in responding to concerns, once you have determined a level of use, you're ready to consider and act on the support needed to sustain or advance implementation. Several possible examples have been provided for you in the decision-making guide (Table 5 on page 81).

- Tell me about [the new practice]. How are you using it [in your classroom; in your work]?

- What do you see as [the new practice's] strengths and weaknesses?

- Give me an example. (Note: This request for information is key in helping to elicit clear descriptions and to help verify actual use. Use it to gain additional clarity.)

- Have you thought about doing things differently with [the new practice]? Tell me about that.

- Do you talk with others about [the new practice]? What do you talk about?

- Have you made recent changes in how you use [the new practice]? What changes have you made and why? Are you considering more?

- Have you received any feedback that affected how you use [the new practice]? Who provided the feedback and what did you do with it?

This time, RIT members should conduct one-legged interviews to help describe the level of use of your improvement or innovation strategy.

Go to the ToolTracker on page 113 to record the RIT's responses to different levels of use. The information gathered here will be useful when responding to concerns about implementation in your school. Refer to Table 5 on the following page for guidance with this process.

Table 5. Decision-making guide for determining levels of use and supporting implementation

Level of Use	Key Decision Question(s)	Listen-for	Sample Actions to Support Use
Mechanical	Have you thought about doing different things with [the new practice]? What changes are you making in your use of [the new practice]?	If changes are primarily to benefit the user, *mechanical use* is likely.	Provide modeling and/or coaching to improve regular, fluid use. Allow opportunities to observe and ask questions of similar users who are routine in their use.
Routine		If no changes are being made, and use is described as uneventful, *routine use* is likely.	This is the initial goal for schools working to ensure greater consistency in implementing adopted routines. Actions to support routine level of use might include celebrating that success, using the teacher/classroom as a model for other users, or prompting them to explore refinements to their practice by consulting a program rubric.
Refinement		If data-driven changes are being made to improve outcomes for students, *refinement use* is likely.	Provide suggestions for thinking about data collection, focusing on how use affects student performance and outcomes. Highlight the use for others as a bright spot worthy of replication.
Integration	Do you have conversations with colleagues about [the new practice]? What things do you talk about?	If changes in use are being made in collaboration with colleagues to improve outcomes for students, *integration use* is likely.	Ensure teachers have sufficient time for collaboration, and explore opportunities to broaden their collaboration with others. Emphasize and support use of inquiry-driven learning through application of improvement cycles (e.g., study-do-reflect-act cycles).
Renewal	Have you thought about replacing or making major changes to [the new practice]?	If considering *major* modifications or other alternatives to the current practice to have an even greater impact on student outcomes, *renewal use* is likely.	If the major changes are truly innovative and align with your plan and vision, support and encourage experimentation. If not, redirect to your plan and existing guidance for implementation.

Change is complex, and as humans, we experience it differently from one another. Even as individuals we can have different responses at different times, depending on the context in which we experience change. For that reason, we're offering quite a few tools to help you recognize and manage the various responses to change you're sure to see as you work to embed improvement efforts in your school.

The next tool offers strategies for helping you frame your message in a way that not only addresses the reasons we know people resist change, but also inspires them (which is to say, intrinsically motivates them) to *want* to change.

We're not suggesting that you use all of these tools all of the time. Rather, view them as a toolkit from which you can draw the tools you need to overcome resistance to change and support your staff through their personal transitions.

Tool #15: Messaging the benefits

The tool below builds on the work of Everett Rogers (2003) to help you enhance the appeal of your change effort by decreasing uncertainty and demonstrating benefits for those who will implement it. As you'll see, this approach to messaging also maps closely onto reasons people resist change, described in Figure 12 on page 74. As an RIT, discuss messaging approaches for each of the five areas.

Compatibility—Connect to your moral purpose
- Show how it's consistent with core values and group norms.
- "We've always said that we want to be more _____."

Advantage—Connect to your vision
- Show how the new approach will make things better.
- "By doing this, we and our students will benefit in the following ways . . ."

Observability—Show how it's working elsewhere
- Visualize success by seeing the success of others doing the same thing.
- "If you want to see it working for others, look no further than . . ."

Simplicity—Connect to your selected innovation
- Make it easy to understand (keep it simple).
- "By doing _____ we'll achieve _____."

Trial-ability—Scaffold new learning
- Give a small opportunity to experiment with something new.
- "Just try this one little first step to see if it works."

Turn to page 114 of the ToolTracker to create an option for each of the messaging approaches. Which might be most useful for staff in your school?

Removing the Threat, Issuing a Challenge

In *Top Dog: The Science of Winning and Losing,* Bronson and Merryman (2013) synthesize numerous studies that show our brains and bodies react quite differently when we experience *threat* conditions. If we fear we're being judged or watched, our brains slow down our decision making and ability to take action. On high alert to avoid mistakes, we actually make *more* of them. For example, when professional soccer players are kicking to win—that is, giving their team a lead in a shootout—they make 92 percent of their goals. But when kicking *not to lose*—when they know a missed goal will cost their team the game—they succeed only 62 percent of the time (Jordet & Hartman, 2008).

In contrast, when we have a "challenge orientation," our brains relax, allowing us to focus less on what might go wrong and more on the task at hand. In sports, athletes play looser and better when playing to win instead of playing not to lose. In academics, anxious C-students become confident A-students. And in organizations, viewing problems as challenges rather than threats can turn risk aversion and anxiety into openness to new ideas, experimentation, and ingenuity.

In many ways, the kind of stress many educators face right now seems to be tantamount to *threat* conditions, which prevent the kind of creative and collaborative thinking most needed to move beyond reliance on simple solutions and toward the sort of deeper analysis and inventive thinking needed to tackle adaptive challenges. Thus, a key takeaway for leaders is to frame any effort not as a threat (*Implement this program or else!*) but as a challenge (*Let's see how many students we can get back on grade level*).

Phase 6: Build a Purposeful Community

How is our culture of inquiry developing?

Creating a Commitment Culture

Janice had forced herself to step back as a leader—sometimes literally, choosing to sit in the back of the room at staff meetings while others took the lead. She had undergone a quiet transformation by challenging herself to view people who were resisting change with more sympathy, considering what emotions might be stirring inside them as they tackled the changes occurring at Stillbrook K–8 School. Mostly, she loved the new energy in her leadership team and in the school. Yet she felt something gnawing at her. She carried the gnawing feeling around with her for several days, agonizing over whether to express it, before finally sharing it with the RIT before the first trimester break.

"So, I don't want to rain on anyone's parade," she announced at the start of the RIT meeting.

"Uh-oh," Belinda said to nervous laughter from the others.

"It's just . . . I've had something on my mind. It's a simple question, really: How are we doing?"

"We're doing great," said Tom enthusiastically. "I've seen amazing things going on in classrooms. Our 6th graders just finished a unit on magnetism that culminated in writing patent applications, complete with diagrams and scientific explanations, for new inventions using magnets."

"We did something similar with the 3rd and 4th graders," Belinda added. "We created a complete history of the county—the geology, flora and fauna, history of first peoples, and more-modern history. Parents were blown away by the book we published. They've been asking for extra copies for grandparents."

"That's great," Janice replied.

"But . . . ?" Belinda asked.

Janice made eye contact with Oscar, who seemed to have the same thing on his mind. "But how is it tied to student success?" he asked quietly.

Janice nodded. "Look, I don't want to be too rigid about this. I love the creativity and excitement I see everywhere, which has probably come about because we're being less dogged about 'teach *this*, like *that*, and track *these* data.' Yet I want to make sure we don't backslide into a free-for-all where we're no longer focused on student learning."

"That's not going to happen," Belinda retorted, sounding agitated. "I mean, it's not happening now. People are working really hard. I've never seen better teaching and student engagement."

"I'm sure that's true," Janice countered. "But how do we *show* that? Not just to the central office, but to ourselves, so we know we're getting better and can find ways to keep getting better—like a scorecard we can point to in staff meetings to chart our progress and identify new goals to aim for."

Belinda exhaled a bit. "OK, sorry if I sounded defensive there. It's just that we've been working hard and getting some great successes. But I agree, let's celebrate those. I think we're saying the same thing."

"I think so, too," Janice agreed.

"So, what would our scorecard look like?" Tom asked.

"There's student achievement data, of course, but that's down the road; we won't take the state test until March or get the results until next August. And anyway, a lot of what we're doing is going way deeper than what kids can show on a bubble sheet. How do we show that?"

"Even before that, there's everything we're doing *right now*," Belinda interjected. "I'm seeing practices changing and kids getting more engaged. I don't have any 'proof' of that yet, but I wish everyone else could see what I'm seeing. If we were a baseball team, I think our batting average would definitely be improving, and the wins would be coming."

"Maybe there are two sets of indicators we ought to track," Oscar offered. "Like how economists track *leading* and *lagging* indicators for the economy. Stuff like retail sales and new business startups are leading indicators that forecast lagging indicators like GDP growth and employment rates. For us, achievement data, especially state test scores, are lagging indicators. But what are our *leading* indicators?"

The group pondered that for a moment.

"Maybe it's embedded in everything we're doing," Tom offered. "Thinking like a scientist here, we're basically testing a hypothesis. We're saying, 'If we give kids more challenging learning tasks, they'll be more engaged—more *curious*—and learn in deeper ways. As a result, their overall achievement will go up.'"

"And they'll stay *curious*, which is a benefit in itself," Belinda added to nods of agreement.

"All right. That's a good place to begin," Oscar interjected.

"So, let's map that out and collect data on each of those points. We can then report on those data in our staff meetings."

"I like where this is going," Janice observed. "We do need some real-time student achievement data, though. We don't want to wait until March—or next August—to confirm or deny our hypothesis. We need something more frequent, like at the end of each learning unit. And we need teacher teams to be looking at real-time data that's meaningful to them in their meetings. Is that possible?"

Tom and Belinda smiled at each other before Belinda responded, "Tom and I will put our heads together about how we can engage teachers in thinking about this question and we'll come back to our next meeting with some ideas."

"That's a good idea," Oscar added. "We could use that to show ourselves that we're improving. I've also been thinking about how we show that we're making changes in the ways we approach teaching, leading, and learning—you know, how we're becoming curious ourselves. I read an article over the weekend about the role leaders have in impacting student achievement. We all know that teachers obviously have the greatest impact, but the article said that leaders influence achievement by creating a strong school culture and climate. It also suggested some ways we can measure culture and climate so we know if we're doing our part to support the changes we want for our school. I'll look into some of those measures and report back at our next meeting."

Janice smiled at the group. "You all are terrific. Look, I know how important it is to have a strong team culture. What's that saying about culture eating strategy for breakfast? Anyway, you all reflect the kind of culture I hope takes hold across the building. Seriously, I feel so fortunate, and grateful, for each and every one of you."

That night, while going through her school mail and messages, Janice found something else for which to be grateful: a notecard from Denise Gray. *Thanks for being a great principal*, it read in Denise's tidy script. Below her signature, she had added a P.S. *I think this is going to work . . . making kids curious.* ∎

Growing a Purposeful Community

Perhaps you've heard the maxim, "Culture eats strategy for breakfast"—possibly coined by management guru Peter Drucker, but used more famously by former Ford Motors CEO Mark Fields—used to emphasize the central role an organization's culture plays in the success of any effort to improve or innovate. Although well-developed strategic plans provide a road map for improvement, it is the culture of a system that either moves innovation forward or hinders its progress. Building and sustaining a high-performance culture is one of the chief responsibilities of leaders and leadership teams.

You may recall learning about five key characteristics of high-poverty, high-performing, "beat-the-odds" schools—those that significantly outperform similar low-performing, high-poverty schools—in Phase 2. These characteristics—shared mission and goals, academic press for achievement, orderly climate, support for teacher influence, and structure—cohere to form a school's culture. The work you have done thus far on your journey has aligned with these characteristics of a high-performance school culture. Your goal during Phase 6 is to measure your progress in fostering these characteristics and building a culture of collaborative inquiry that results in continuously improving outcomes for all students.

Through the preceding phases of your journey you have:

- Clarified your moral purpose and vision.

- Established common processes and approaches to professional learning and peer coaching that reflect high expectations for all.

- Marshaled your resources and energy to identify and focus on what matters most.

- Worked to effectively respond to the challenges of change, including meeting individuals where they are in the change process.

- Made it possible for teachers to have greater influence over their own learning and professional practice.

In doing so, you have provided the support and encouragement needed to alleviate individual concerns and strengthen professional practice, helping to build a common sense of hope and belief that you can make a difference for students. In short, you have begun to grow a *purposeful community*, "one with the collective efficacy and capability to develop and use assets to accomplish goals that matter to all community members through agreed-upon processes" (Marzano, Waters, & McNulty, 2005, p. 99).

The central question for Phase 6 is: What progress are we making toward developing a positive, inquiry-driven school culture?

Starting with the core of the graphic in Figure 15, you should have a good sense of how the purpose, values, and vision you clarified at the beginning of this process have resonated and captured the hearts of your staff. Are you hearing them talk about their work with curiosity and reinvigorated interest and energy? Have you walked into the teachers' lounge to hear staff asking questions about their work and sharing their experiences with others?

Moving out one ring to "agreed-upon processes," how are you doing with implementing the professional learning design principles? At this point, you could return to the do-confirm

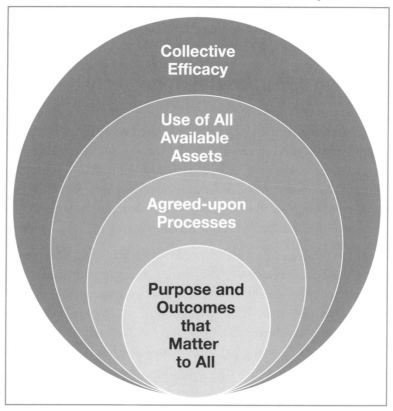

Figure 15. Characteristics of a purposeful community

checklist on pages 62–63 and reassess your progress with each principle. This will also serve to remind you of what next steps may be necessary to progress further toward ideal implementation. With respect to peer coaching, are teachers becoming more comfortable opening their classrooms to peer observers? Are they consistently applying rapid cycles of improvement and innovation to the study of their professional practice?

To explore how well you've been using all available assets, you might begin by returning to the bright spots you identified during Phase 2 and the conditions you identified that were in place to support their use. These conditions, or assets, are ones that can often be leveraged to strengthen and move implementation forward. Which of these assets are key to the success of your area of focus? What other assets—both tangible and intangible—are supporting your teacher teams in deepening their professional inquiry?

The fourth component of a purposeful community, collective efficacy, has the potential to be a game changer. Research has found collective efficacy—the belief that we, as a whole, can behave in ways needed to benefit student outcomes—to be a strong predictor of student achievement (Bandura, 1993; Goddard, Hoy, & Hoy, 2000; Goddard, LoGerfo, & Hoy, 2004; Goddard, Goddard, & Tschannen-Moran, 2007), even when accounting for differences in student background and prior achievement. That is, a faculty of teachers with a strong sense of collective efficacy is more likely to produce positive student outcomes than a faculty without these shared beliefs (Goddard, Goddard, Kim, & Miller, 2015).

Leadership and School Achievement

Second only to teaching, school leadership improves student achievement the most, primarily through the support leaders provide for teachers (Leithwood, Louis, Anderson, & Wahlstrom, 2004). Leaders who frequently monitor instruction and provide strong instructional supports have schools with teachers who are more likely involved in high levels of collaborative work focused on improving instruction (Goddard et al., 2015). Moreover, Goddard and colleagues found that in schools where teacher collaboration focused on instructional improvement, collective efficacy beliefs were stronger. Thus, by promoting a culture of collaboration focused on the improvement of instruction, school leaders (and school leadership teams like your RIT) have a greater likelihood of influencing collective efficacy and student achievement (Goddard et al., 2007, 2015; Louis, Dretzke, & Wahlstrom, 2009).

So, what does all of this mean? For starters, you should begin to see (and measure) a growing sense of collective efficacy in schools where leaders emphasize teacher collaboration and collaborative work—just as you have done in the phases of your improvement and innovation journey thus far. There are several sources for potential measures of collective efficacy. At the time of this writing, one good (and free!) one is on the website of Megan Tschannen-Moran: http://wmpeople.wm.edu/site/page/mxtsch/researchtools.

One additional component of culture related to student achievement is school climate. In 2013, McREL and collaborator Roger Goddard developed a survey of teachers' perceptions of school climate and studied its predictive validity for grade 5 literacy achievement in Australian schools. Findings revealed that 75% of the variance in literacy achievement among schools could be predicted by the way teachers reported feeling about school climate. Additional analysis showed that school leadership facilitated better teacher collaboration and promoted academic optimism, including collective efficacy, resulting in improved literacy achievement. Thus, a leadership focus on improving and supporting high-quality teacher collaboration may serve to foster collective efficacy and improve student achievement and outcomes.

Many schools and districts already employ measures of school climate that can be used to keep your RIT informed about its development. The National Center on Safe and Supportive Learning Environments (NCSSLE) maintains an updated compendium of school climate measures for students, family, and school staff, some of which are available without charge. The free U.S. Department of Education School Climate Survey (EDSCLS) listed on the site is appropriate for grade 5–12 students, staff, and parents. The survey and survey platform are maintained and updated regularly. The EDSCLS platform and other survey information may be accessed as of this writing at: https://safesupportivelearning.ed.gov/topic-research/school-climate-measurement/school-climate-survey-compendium.

Finally, it's important to note that while you and your RIT must work on building a positive school culture and climate, it's not done in isolation from the real work of improvement—namely, improving teaching and learning, and supporting student success. In other words, a great school culture will get you nowhere if no one knows where you're going or what role each member of the school community must play to get there.

Tool #16: Characteristics of a purposeful community

Ask each RIT member to individually reflect on each characteristic of a purposeful community by responding to the directions and prompts provided below. You'll notice that a purposeful community is really the culmination of many other conversations you've already had.

Purpose and outcomes that matter to all

Review the work and statements regarding your shared values, purpose, and vision developed and refined in Phase 1. List 3–5 key ideas:

1. _____

2. _____

3. _____

4. _____

5. _____

- What are you hearing teachers and staff talking about related to your values, purpose, and vision?

  _____

  _____

- What classroom evidence can you point to that reflects a shared sense of your values, purpose, and vision?

  _____

  _____

Agreed-upon processes

Review the principles for peer coaching (Table 4, page 65).

- Are teachers becoming more comfortable in opening their classrooms to peer observers? What supports do they need to make progress?

  _____

  _____

- Are teachers consistently applying rapid cycles of improvement and innovation to the study of their professional practice? What supports do they need to make progress?

  _____

  _____

  _____

Use of all available assets

Review the bright spots you identified during Phase 2 and the conditions you found to be important in supporting the implementation of these bright spots.

- What conditions, or assets, are you using to strengthen and deepen implementation of bright spots in your focus area?

_____

_____

- What other assets (tangible and intangible) can be leveraged to support teachers in deepening their professional inquiry and growing their professional practice?

_____

_____

Collective efficacy

- What measure of collective efficacy will you use to monitor changes over time?

_____

_____

- What examples of teacher collaboration resulting in positive student achievement can you describe?

_____

_____

- What measure of school climate will you use to monitor changes over time?

_____

_____

- What examples of a positively developing school climate, especially with respect to teacher collaboration, have you noticed developing in your school?

_____

_____

Now, turn to pages 115–116 of the ToolTracker and, as a group this time, discuss and record key reflections on the characteristics of a purposeful community and your journey thus far.

Building Momentum with a "Commitment Culture"

Ultimately, the whole inside-out process is designed to help you to create a school that feels less like a slow-moving bureaucracy and more like a Silicon Valley startup, where people engage in rapid-cycle improvement efforts. If that seems like a stretch given that most schools are public institutions hemmed in with rules and regulations, consider the research of Stanford's Baron & Hannan (2002), who tracked the performance of 200 Silicon Valley startup companies to see if different types of organizational cultures predicted success. They found the companies mostly fit into five models, or approaches to selecting, motivating, and coordinating talent:

- **Star** model. These companies hired broadly talented, high-potential people from selective universities, gave them interesting work, and let them operate with a great deal of autonomy.

- **Engineering** model. These companies hired technically skilled people, gave them interesting work, and kept them "plied with enough sugar and caffeine to stay energized" (p. 14).

- **Commitment** model. Considered quaint and outdated in Silicon Valley, these companies hired team-oriented people who fit the culture and motivated them with a sense of building something big together.

- **Bureaucracy** model. These companies hired skilled people, put them on projects that matched their skills, and managed them through formal processes and structures.

- **Autocratic** model. These companies hired technically skilled people, motivated them with financial incentives, and managed them closely, often under the founder's watchful eye.

The researchers found that star model companies tended to grow fast, but often hit a wall, likely due to infighting stemming from resentment of the stars' *prima donna* behavior. The engineering and bureaucracy models had fair to middling performance, and autocratic companies fared the worst, being most prone to go out of business.

Of all these models, only one proved consistently effective: the commitment model. Commitment companies were more resilient and faster-moving, with less administrative oversight. Consider what that means. At the heart of the most successful Silicon Valley startup companies isn't money, hard-charging egos, or do-as-I-say edicts. Rather, it's a *commitment* to shared purpose, values, and vision. And thus, we come full circle back to where we began this guidebook, an idea that's as relevant to schools as to startups: creating a culture that's committed to moral purpose, shared values, and a clear vision for change.

As we noted at the beginning, this guidebook has been designed for anyone who seeks to make a lasting change in their schools—that is, for anyone who wants to serve as an architect of a *commitment culture*. Now that you're equipped with a blueprint and pathways for change, your redesign need not take years. Rather, you can take actions today that will have immediate benefits for your students, while generating improvements for your teachers and students that will endure well into the future.

Epilogue: Reflect and Celebrate

What have we accomplished together? What challenges will we tackle next?

Seeing a Metamorphosis

As Janice walked to the school library, heading toward her last RIT meeting of the year, she found herself smiling. For the first time—ever, perhaps—she'd felt energy in the building all through May and into early June. Instead of limping to the finish line, teachers and students were sprinting to the end, engaged in a big effort called a "Curiosity Convention," in which students displayed their in-depth science and research projects. Teachers were looking at data they'd gathered themselves from their common assessments and were using those to make real-time adjustments to their teaching. They were also abuzz with new things they were curious about and wanted to start working on next year, like asking better questions in the classroom and developing robust profiles of every student, so they could get to know them academically and personally.

As she passed Denise Gray's room, she found her taking down her bulletin boards. Janice stepped inside and closed the door. "How are you doing?" she asked.

Denise's eyes were moist. "Well, I never thought this day would come, but it's here."

Janice gave Denise a quick hug. "You'll be missed."

"I want to thank you for something," Denise said, dabbing her eyes with a tissue. "Thank you for not giving up on me. I know that . . . well, I can be curmudgeonly at times. And

this last year was really hard on me. A lot of the stuff we were doing didn't make sense to me at first. I kept thinking the problem isn't *me*: I haven't changed, it's the students who have changed, so why do I need to entertain them? And then it hit me: I *hadn't* changed, but I needed to. My kids needed me to. When I came to that realization, I threw myself into the whole idea of challenging learning tasks and I've seen lightbulbs turn on for kids like I've never seen before. I've become the best teacher of my career—40 years in."

"I don't suppose I could coax you into staying one more year?" Janice asked, repeating a request she'd made many times before.

"No, I have promises to keep, and miles to go before I sleep," Denise said, quoting Robert Frost.

"I am serious about you getting on the substitute teachers list, though," Janice added. "You'll be my first choice every time."

"I think I'd like that," Denise replied. "Besides, this old thorn might not know what to do with herself if she wasn't stuck in someone's side," she added, giving Janice a gentle poke.

They both laughed and Janice left the room. When she entered the library, her team was laughing and sharing a plate of cookies. The mood felt celebratory—a 180-degree change from a year earlier.

"Well, gang," Janice said. "We have a few housekeeping items to cover today, but first, I want to ask you something: Where are we in our story? If someone were writing the story of us in a book, what chapter would we be in right now?"

The group fell silent. Janice grabbed a cookie and let them ruminate. Tom, who had been writing in his notepad, looked up. "I'd say our story's not done, not by a long shot. But I feel like—and maybe this is because I'm thinking about my summer vacation—but I feel like we've been hiking up a mountain and have finally gotten to our first vista point, where we can look out and say, 'Wow. This is pretty amazing.' There's a new vibe around the school now. Yeah, there are still some stragglers not quite up the hill, but they're starting to come along with us."

"I always like your metaphors, Tom," said Belinda. "I was imagining writing a play about us—I think it would be a good one. OK, so it might be off-off-Broadway," she added to chuckles from the group. "Nonetheless, there's been quite an arc to our story. Last year was *dark*—sort of like the part of a play right before intermission where everything has gone wrong and you're not sure how the protagonists will get out of the mess they're in. And then we started to find our way out. Not to be too much of an armchair psychologist, but something changed with *us*. Janice bravely stepped back and forced all of us to step up. Now, I feel like things are really coming together for us as a team. Oh, and teachers are acting totally different, too. They're not so walled off now and they're realizing that the answers to any challenge are almost always in the building. Somewhere, someone is doing something that can solve the problem."

"I agree," said Oscar. "It feels like we're a winning team again. You know that feeling? Like when you go into every game feeling, not *cocky,* but confident. Here's what I wrote in my notes." Oscar held up his notepad:

Doing ⟶ Inquiring

"Like any winning team, we've learned to reflect," he continued. "We go back to the game tape and study it. That's made it easier to discard old practices and adopt new ones. We've been seeing roadblocks and impediments—how our past practices have gotten in the way. For me, I've come to a whole new realization of what it means to be data-driven. It's not just about how the *kids* are doing, but it's also about *us* and what *we* can do better."

"And Janice, what about you?" Belinda asked. "Where do you see us?"

"Well, you know I took a bunch of business classes in college so I've been thinking about Jim Collins' flywheel concept—you know, the idea that in the factories of old there was this large wheel in the center of the plant that generated all the plant's energy. Getting it started was slow and arduous, but as it gained momentum, it spun faster and faster until it almost seemed to spin by itself, in perpetual motion. I think our flywheel is spinning now. I can't say exactly what push got it there, but I guess that's the point. It was a whole bunch of little pushes, by everyone, that has helped it to spin."

Janice paused. Suddenly, she felt emotional; something significant had occurred at Stillbrook K–8 School.

"I'm so proud of everyone here," she said finally. "Other people across the district are hearing about what we're doing and asking me how I created such an innovative school, which is funny for me, because I don't feel like a very creative or innovative person. After all"—she looked down at her outfit—"I'm wearing the same clothes I had 10 years ago. But here we are, an *innovative* school. We've climbed out of the valley, we're in the second act of our play, we're on a winning streak. Whichever metaphor you prefer, thank you, everyone." ■

Steering Clear of Implementation Dips

Stillbrook's story reflects one journey a school might take; yours might look different. Maybe things still aren't going smoothly—maybe you're still stuck in the valley or in the first act of your play. That's OK. Remember, whether you're establishing new routines, encouraging collegial collaboration, or supporting rapid-cycle innovation, you're asking people to change their habits, and old habits die hard—even when we *want* to change them.

Think of the last time you tried to adopt a new diet or exercise routine and how easy it was to slide back to your old ways. School change is similar—only it's dozens of people trying to change their habits all at once. Fortunately, one thing we know about changing habits is that it's much easier to do with others—that's why people join diet clubs, gym classes, and religious organizations. We need each other to get better.

When you're trying to change habits on a large scale it's normal to experience a phenomenon often known as the "implementation dip," a term coined by Canadian researcher Michael Fullan (2001), who observed that when the fear of change collides with lack of know-how, performance tends to slump.

Figure 16. The implementation dip

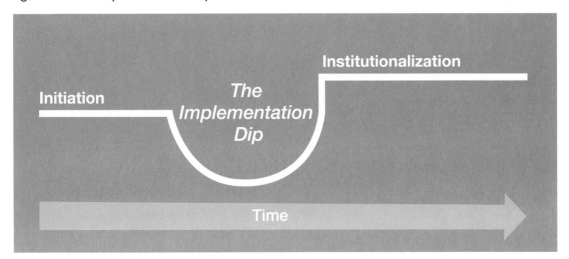

To overcome implementation dips, Fullan encourages schools and their leaders to:

- Maintain focus and urgency to quash "this too shall pass" syndrome.

- Monitor implementation to avoid backsliding into familiar yet inferior practices.

- Listen to naysayers and, as appropriate, incorporate their ideas into change efforts.

- Work as teams to buck each other up when the going gets tough.

These strategies can help your RIT overcome implementation dips and begin to experience success. Early on, it's especially important that you chart your progress and celebrate every success, even small ones, because doing so builds the can-do attitude and sense of momentum people need to keep pushing themselves harder.

Now that you've completed one cycle of inquiry-driven professional learning focused on what matters most to you right now, a new culture of curiosity and inside-out change should be starting to take hold. Take a moment to celebrate your success with your team and your school before returning to Phase 2 to identify your next steps to innovation and engage in the cycle again, continuing your improvement and innovation journey.

Final Reflection Questions

Return to the ToolTracker one more time, using Tool #17 on page 117 to reflect on your journey.

- Imagine your school having the same sort of celebration as Stillbrook K–8 School. What will you have done to get there? What will be different about your culture? Your focus? Your interactions as a team?

- What has surprised you about the steps along this improvement and innovation journey?

- What key takeaways or lessons learned would you share with your colleagues in other schools regarding the six phases of the journey?

- Where does your journey take you next?

Enjoy Your Journey—and Send Us a Postcard

Ultimately, school improvement is a journey—a never-ending one at that. Every school is different, of course, so there's no lockstep program or series of simple steps you can follow to move from improvement to innovation. Thus, the tools and advice we offer in this guidebook are by no means the final word; rather, we hope they serve as starting points and mileposts for your journey. Change, especially change worth making, is often a "messy" process. It can feel at times like you're taking two steps forward and one step back. The important thing is that you keep moving forward.

Leadership is a journey, too. We hope this guidebook has stretched your thinking as a leader—no matter what formal title you have in your school or school system. Just as teachers need others to help them change old habits and adopt new ones, leaders do, too—and change is always easier when we change alongside others. So, we encourage you to work with other leaders in your school or a network of leaders from outside your school who will challenge your thinking, inspire you with new ideas, and help you hold yourself accountable for becoming the best leader you can be.

Finally, as members of a profession, we remind you to share with others beyond your own school and system. Share your journey of improvement and innovation by presenting at conferences, writing articles for journals, and networking with schools in other districts in your region. We'd also love to know how you're doing. Tell us where you've experienced challenges and successes, and what you've learned along the way. We'll be energized to hear your story, so please keep in touch by sending us some "postcards" of your journey, and we will do the same.

Bon voyage!

Let's continue this conversation!

Reach the authors and other experts at McREL who are exploring the power of curiosity, just like you are.

800.858.6830 | www.mcrel.org | info@mcrel.org

Tool #1: Identifying shared values (p. 12)

List your 3–7 core and/or aspirational values on the left, and a memorable word or phrase associated with each value on the right.

Core/aspirational values	Memorable word/phrase

Tool #2: Finding shared moral purpose (p. 15)

Complete the following sentence stem to state your shared moral purpose.

At _____,

we believe _____

_____

_____

_____

_____

_____

_____

_____

_____

_____

_____

_____

Tool #3: Framing your vision (p. 18)

Record one or two framing statements that best describe your vision. The statement(s) should be brief in order to consistently and continuously remind the entire community where you are going.

Tool #4: Data springboard (pp. 24–25)

A data-informed picture of your current reality.

Types of data reviewed: _____

Demographic: _____

Perception: _____

Performance: _____

Program: _____

Impressions based on data: _____

_____

Ways in which our data and impressions align with our stated purpose and vision:

_____

_____

Ways in which our data diverge from our stated purpose and vision:

_____

_____

What will our school look like when our data and outcomes align with our purpose and vision?

- What will have changed for students? _____

_____

- What changes in teaching will we see? _____

_____

- What changes in learning will we see? _____

_____

- How will we feel about ourselves? _____

_____

- How will we feel about our students? _____

_____

- What will have changed about us as an organization? _____

_____

- What other (even less tangible) benefits might we experience? _____

_____

Tool #5: Applying asset-based thinking to school challenges (p. 28)

For this tool, consider one of the challenges that emerged from your data.

- What challenge did you identify?

- What positive elements related to this challenge did you identify?

- What actions or conditions did you identify that created or contributed to the positive elements you identified?

- What themes or patterns do you see in the actions or conditions that supported the development of the positive elements you identified?

- What opportunities exist to replicate and scale these actions and conditions so that this challenge is effectively addressed by others who encounter it?

Tool #6: Using instructional rounds to find bright spots (p. 31)

After you have completed an instructional rounds cycle, record the following information.

Focus for visit: _____

Observers' comments about:

- Affirmations (strategies to keep using):

  _____

  _____

- Reflections (strategies to reconsider):

  _____

  _____

- Considerations (strategies you'd like to try):

  _____

  _____

What conditions did the team identify as necessary to replicate (and potentially scale) the bright spots?

_____

_____

_____

What five key messages about your school—its challenges and bright spots—should everyone in your community know?

1. _____

2. _____

3. _____

4. _____

5. _____

Tool #7: What Matters Most improvement and innovation pathways (p. 39)

In the table below, place an X in the boxes to reflect where you placed your school on the pathway for each What Matters Most component.

	Adopt better routines	Ensure greater consistency	Develop collegial expertise	Foster shared innovation
Curricular pathways to success				
Challenging, engaging, and intentional instruction				
Whole-child student supports				
High-performance school culture				
Data-driven, high-reliability systems				

Continued on next page

Tool #7 (*cont.*): What Matters Most improvement and innovation pathways

Now, record the bright spots, potential areas for improvement and innovation, and any additional data needs you identified.

	Bright spots ★	Possible areas for improvement and innovation !	Additional data needed ▲
Curricular pathways to success			
Challenging, engaging, and intentional instruction			
Whole-child student supports			
High-performance school culture			
Data-driven, high-reliability systems			

Based on your pathways assessment and discussion of bright spots and needs, which component of the What Matters Most framework did your RIT determine you should focus on? Remember to pay close attention to areas where you have not yet adopted or ensured consistency in routines.

Our selected What Matters Most focus:

- ☐ Curricular pathways to success
- ☐ Challenging, engaging, and intentional instruction
- ☐ Whole-child student supports
- ☐ High-performance school culture
- ☐ Data-driven, high-reliability systems

Tool #8: Finding your focus (p. 45)

School snapshot: Using the What Matters Most component you've identified as your focus, what will you do to make a difference in your school's outcomes?

What are the opportunities for growth within this What Matters Most component that are best aligned with your school's purpose and vision?

_____

_____

_____

Use the following prompts to generate a shared understanding of how you'd like to focus your efforts:

- What do we want?

_____

_____

- For whom do we want it?

_____

_____

- By when do we want it?

_____

_____

- What is our measure of success?

_____

_____

- Why is this important to our school?

_____

_____

_____

_____

Tool #9: Telling your story (p. 47)

Use this space to tell a compelling, shared narrative for your improvement and innovation journey.

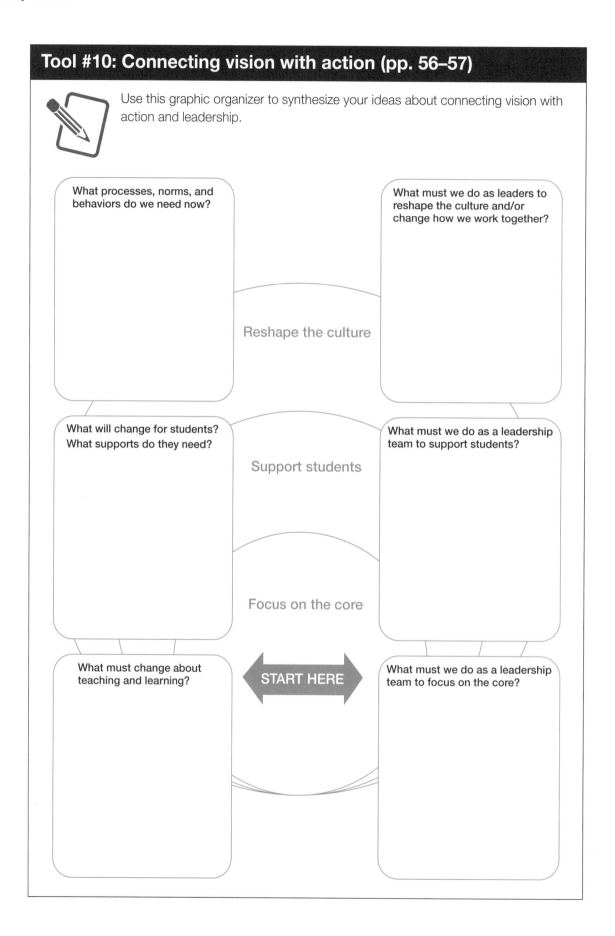

Tool #10: Connecting vision with action (pp. 56–57)

Use this graphic organizer to synthesize your ideas about connecting vision with action and leadership.

What processes, norms, and behaviors do we need now?

What must we do as leaders to reshape the culture and/or change how we work together?

Reshape the culture

What will change for students? What supports do they need?

What must we do as a leadership team to support students?

Support students

Focus on the core

What must change about teaching and learning?

START HERE

What must we do as a leadership team to focus on the core?

Tool #11: Assess your professional learning needs (pp. 62–63)

Based on your review of the Professional Learning Design Principles, what three actions did your RIT decide would have the greatest impact on professional learning in your school? List your three actions and some preliminary thoughts about how you might advance these actions in your school here:

1. _____

_____

_____

_____

2. _____

_____

_____

_____

3. _____

_____

_____

_____

Tool #12: Directive versus empowering leadership styles (p. 73)

Record your response to these questions:

Are the demands of this stage primarily associated with technical solutions or adaptive challenges? List your challenges and identify each as technical or adaptive.

_____

_____

_____

_____

_____

_____

Do you know what to do and just need to do it, or does the road ahead require a more complex approach? Make some notes about new learning that might be required to address your challenges.

_____

_____

_____

_____

_____

Tool #13: One-legged interview to identify concerns (p. 78)

 In this activity, picture yourself in the role of an RIT member whose school is working on increasing use of higher-order, curiosity-provoking questions in the classroom. When you visit with teachers around the building, asking, "How are you doing with asking students more higher-level questions?" you hear a range of concerns, listed below. Using the major clusters of concern from page 77, determine the kind of concern most likely being expressed.

Response	Unconcern	Self	Task	Impact
Marta: *Well, I wasn't at the last staff meeting, but James gave me the handouts. I'm focused on planning for our spring science fair right now. I'll take a look at that information once the fair is done.*				
Colleen: *I found this book about ways to add better questions to your lessons. My question is how I am supposed to take these specific question examples and make them fit my lessons. I feel like I need a recipe for how to do it.*				
Kevin: *You know I've been teaching math for a long time and my students typically do pretty well. It's hard for me to think about doing things different, you know?*				
Tasha: *I have written questions at different levels for each lesson. It was fun coming up with all of them, but I'm having some trouble figuring out exactly where to fit them in and still get through the lesson.*				
Randall: *I've started asking at least three additional higher-order questions in each lesson and I'm so impressed with the responses from my students! They are proving they know more than I realized!*				
Dominique: *I've been asking questions at the beginning of each lesson to capture students' curiosity – things like "Suppose you want to buy a new car. Would it cost you less to buy it from a car dealer here, or fly to Japan, where the car is made, buy it, and transport it here?" Students have been so engaged.*				
Eric: *Sara, Talia, and I have partnered to write questions for specific purposes in our lessons. On Tuesday, they came in while I was teaching and recorded all the questions I asked, and the kinds of responses students gave. Today we're going to meet to talk about what they observed and refine our questions so they can use them next.*				

Continued on next page

Tool #13 (*cont.*): One-legged interview to identify concerns (p. 78)

Now, have each of your RIT members engage in one-legged interviews focused on your improvement and innovation effort with 5–10 staff over the course of one week. At your next RIT meeting, tally the clusters of concern in the following table. Then, identify actions that you can take to support individuals with their concerns. Commit to practicing these responses as you continue to talk to staff about concerns.

Primary concerns expressed	Number of staff	Action to support staff and respond to concerns
Unconcern		
Self		
Task		
Impact		

Tool #14: One-legged interview to identify use (p. 80)

Similar to the exercise with concerns, have each RIT member engage in one-legged interviews focused on your improvement and innovation effort with 5–10 staff over the course of one week. At your next RIT meeting, tally the determinations of level of use in the following table. Then, identify actions that you can take to support individuals in their use. Commit to practicing these actions as you continue to talk to staff about use.

Level of use	Number of staff	Action to support use
Mechanical		
Routine		
Refinement		
Integration		
Renewal		

Tool #15: Messaging the benefits (p. 83)

 Create an option for each of the messaging approaches below that speaks to the heads and hearts of your staff. Remember to focus on "What's in it for me?" You may create your own message from scratch, or use the starter to help get you going.

Compatibility—Connect to your moral purpose. Show how it's consistent with core values and group norms. Sample starter: *We've always said that we want to be...*

Your *Compatibility* message:

_____

_____

Advantage—Connect to your vision. Show how the new approach will make things better. Sample starter: *By doing this, we and our students will...*

Your *Advantage* message:

_____

_____

Observability—Describe the focus of change. Visualize success by seeing the success of others doing the same thing. Sample starter: *If you want to see it working for others...*

Your *Observability* message:

_____

_____

Simplicity—Connect to your selected theory of action. Make it easy to understand (keep it simple). Sample starter: *By doing _____ we will...*

Your *Simplicity* message:

_____

_____

Trial-ability—Scaffold new learning. Give a small opportunity to experiment with something new. Sample starter: *Have you tried _____ to see how it works?*

Your *Trial-ability* message:

_____

_____

Tool #16: Characteristics of a purposeful community (pp. 90–91)

Use your individual reflections from pages 90–91 to complete this as a group.

Purpose and outcomes that matter to all

Review the work and statements regarding your shared values, purpose, and vision developed and refined in Phase 1. List 3–5 key ideas.

1. _____
2. _____
3. _____
4. _____
5. _____

- What are you hearing teachers and staff talking about related to your values, purpose, and vision? _____

_____

_____

- What classroom evidence can you point to that reflects a shared sense of your values, purpose, and vision? _____

_____

_____

Agreed-upon processes

Review the Principles for Peer Coaching (Table 4, page 65).

- Are teachers becoming more comfortable in opening their classrooms to peer observers? _____

_____

_____

What supports do they need to make progress? _____

_____

- Are teachers consistently applying rapid cycles of improvement and innovation to the study of their professional practice? _____

_____

_____

What supports do they need to make progress? _____

_____

_____

Continued on next page

Tool #16 (*cont.*): Characteristics of a purposeful community (pp. 90–91)

Use of all available assets

Review the bright spots you identified during Phase 2 and the conditions you found to be important in supporting the implementation of these bright spots.

- What conditions, or assets, are you using to strengthen and deepen implementation of bright spots in your focus area?

  _____

  _____

  _____

- What other assets (tangible and intangible) can be leveraged to support teachers in deepening their professional inquiry and growing their professional practice?

  _____

  _____

  _____

Collective efficacy

- What measure of collective efficacy will you use to monitor changes over time?

  _____

  _____

- What examples of teacher collaboration resulting in positive student achievement can you describe?

  _____

  _____

  _____

- What measure of school climate will you use to monitor changes over time?

  _____

  _____

  _____

- What examples of a positively developing school climate, especially with respect to teacher collaboration, have you noticed developing in your school?

  _____

  _____

  _____

Tool #17: Final reflection questions (p. 96)

Final reflection questions:

Reflect on your journey thus far by considering and responding to the following questions:

- Imagine your school having the same sort of celebration as Stillbrook. What will you have done to get there? What will be different about your culture? Your focus? Your interactions as a team?

_____

_____

_____

_____

- What has surprised you about the steps along this improvement and innovation journey?

_____

_____

_____

_____

- What key takeaways or lessons learned would you share with your colleagues in other schools regarding the six phases of the journey?

_____

_____

_____

_____

_____

- Where does your journey take you next?

_____

_____

_____

_____

_____

References

Bandura, A. (1977). Self-efficacy: Toward a unifying theory of behavioral change. *Psychological Review, 84*, 191–215.

Bandura, A. (1986). *Social foundations of thought and action: A social cognitive theory.* Englewood Cliffs, NJ: Prentice Hall.

Bandura, A. (1993). Perceived self-efficacy in cognitive development and functioning. *Educational Psychologist, 28*, 117–48.

Bandura, A. (1997). *Self-efficacy: The exercise of control.* New York: Freeman.

Barber, M., & Mourshed, M. (2007). *How the world's best-performing school systems come out on top.* London: McKinsey and Company.

Baron, J. N., & Hannan, M. T. (2002). Organizational blueprints for success in high-tech start-ups: Lessons from the Stanford project on emerging companies. *California Management Review, 44*(3), 8–36.

Bezzina, M. (2007). Moral purpose and shared leadership: The leaders transforming learning and learners pilot study. *Australian Council for Educational Research.* Retrieved from http://research. acer.edu.au/cgi/viewcontent.cgi?article=1013&context=research_conference_2007

Bridges, W. (2009). *Managing transitions: Making the most of change* (3rd ed.). Boston, MA: Da Capo Press.

Brinson, D., Kowal, J., & Hassel, B. C. (2008). *School turnarounds: Actions and results.* Lincoln, IL: Center on Innovation & Improvement.

Bronson, P., & Merryman, A. (2013). *Top dog: The science of winning and losing.* New York: Twelve.

Carson, J. B., Tesluk, P. E., & Marrone, J. A. (2007). Shared leadership in teams: An investigation of antecedent conditions and performance. *Academy of Management Journal, 50*(5), 1217–1234.

City, E. A., Elmore, R. F., Fiarman, S. E., & Teitel, L. (2009). *Instructional rounds in education: A network approach to improving teaching and learning.* Cambridge, MA: Harvard Education Press.

Dean, C. B., Hubbell, E. R., Pitler, H., & Stone, B. (2012). *Classroom instruction that works* (2nd ed.). Alexandria, VA: ASCD.

Deutschman, A. (2006). *Change or die: Three keys to change at work and in life.* New York: Harper Business.

Fullan, M. (2001). *Leading in a culture of change.* San Francisco: Jossey-Bass.

George, A. A., Hall, G. E., & Stiegelbauer, S. M. (2006). *Measuring implementation in schools: The stages of concern questionnaire.* Austin, TX: SEDL.

Goddard, R. D., Hoy, W. K., & Hoy, A. W. (2000). Collective teacher efficacy: Its meaning, measure, and effect on student achievement. *American Education Research Journal, 37*(2), 479–507.

Goddard, R. D., LoGerfo, L., & and Hoy, W. K. (2004). High school accountability: The role of collective efficacy. *Educational Policy, 18*(3), 403–25.

Goddard, R. D., Goddard, Y. L., Kim, E. S., & Miller, R. (2015). A theoretical and empirical analysis of the roles of instructional leadership, teacher collaboration, and collective efficacy beliefs in support of student learning. *American Journal of Education, 121*(4), 501–530.

Goddard, Y. L., Goddard, R. D., & Tschannen-Moran, M. (2007). A theoretical and empirical investigation of teacher collaboration for school improvement and student achievement in public elementary schools. *Teachers College Record, 109*(4), 877–96.

Goodwin, B. (2011). *Simply better: Doing what matters most to change the odds of student success.* Alexandria, VA: ASCD.

Goodwin, B. (2015). Getting unstuck. *Educational Leadership, 72*(9), 8–12.

Goodwin, B. (2017). Personalization and failing forward. *Educational Leadership, 74*(6), 80–81.

Goodwin, B., Cameron, G., & Hein, H. (2015). *Balanced leadership for powerful learning: Tools for achieving success in your school.* Alexandria, VA: ASCD.

Hall, G. E., Dirksen, D. J., & George, A. A. (2006). *Measuring implementation in schools: Levels of use.* Austin, TX: SEDL.

Hall, G. E., & Hord, S. M. (1987). *Change in schools: Facilitating the process.* Albany, NY: State University of New York Press.

Hall, G. E., & Hord, S. M. (2015). *Implementing change: Patterns, principles, and potholes* (4th ed.). Upper Saddle River, NJ: Pearson Education.

Heath, C., & Heath, D. (2010). *Switch: How to change things when change is hard.* New York: Crown Business.

Heifetz, R. A., & Laurie, D. L. (1997). The work of leadership. *Harvard Business Review, 75*(1), 124–134.

Hopkins, D. (2011). *Powerful learning: taking educational reform to scale.* Melbourne, Australia: Education Policy and Research Division, Office for Policy, Research and Innovation, Victoria Department of Education and Early Childhood Development.

Hopkins, D. (2016). *Models of practice.* Denver, CO: McREL International.

Hopkins, D., & Craig, W. (2011). Going deeper: From the inside out. In D. Hopkins, J. Munro, & W. Craig (Eds.), *Powerful learning: A strategy for systemic educational improvement,* 153–172. Camberwell, Australia: Australian Council for Educational Research Press.

Hopkins, D., & Craig, W. (2015). *Leadership for powerful learning.* Denver, CO: McREL International.

Hopkins, D., & Craig, W., with Knight, O. (2015). *Curiosity and powerful learning.* Denver, CO: McREL International.

Hoy, W. K., Tarter, C. J., & Hoy, A. W. (2006). Academic optimism of schools: A force for student achievement. *American Educational Research Journal, 43*(3), 440.

Jordet, G., & Hartman, E. (2008). Avoidance motivation and choking under pressure in soccer penalty shootouts. *Journal of Sport & Exercise Psychology, 30*(4), 450–457.

Joyce, B., & Showers, B. (2002). *Student achievement through staff development* (3rd ed.). Alexandria, VA: ASCD.

Kamenetz, A., & Turner, C. (2016, October). *The high school graduation rate reaches a record high—again.* Retrieved from http://www.npr.org/sections/ed/2016/10/17/498246451/the-high-school-graduation-reaches-a-record-high-again

Kashdan, T. B., & Roberts, J. E. (2004). Trait and state curiosity in the genesis of intimacy: Differentiation from related constructs. *Journal of Social and Clinical Psychology, 23*(6), 792-816.

Kashdan, T. B., & Steger, M. F. (2007). Curiosity and pathways to well-being and meaning in life: Traits, states, and everyday behaviors. *Motivation and Emotion, 31*(3), 159-173.

Lencioni, P. (2002, July). Make your values mean something. *Harvard Business Review.* Retrieved from https://hbr.org/2002/07/make-your-values-mean-something

Leithwood, K., Louis, K. S., Anderson, S., & Wahlstrom, K. (2004). *How leadership influences student learning.* New York: Wallace Foundation.

Louis, K. S., Dretzke, B., & Wahlstrom, K. (2009, April). *How does leadership affect student achievement? Results from a national survey.* Paper presented at the annual meeting of the American Educational Research Association, San Diego.

Lorinkova, N., Pearsall, M., & Sims, H. (2013). Examining the differential longitudinal performance of directive versus empowering leadership in teams. *Academy of Management, 56*(2), 573–596.

Marzano, R. J., Waters, T., & McNulty, B. (2005). *School leadership that works: From research to results.* Alexandria, VA: Association for Supervision and Curriculum Development.

Maslow, A. H. (1943). A theory of human motivation. *Psychological Review, 50*(4), 370-96.

McREL (2005). *McREL Insights: Schools that "beat the odds."* Aurora, CO: Author.

Newell, A., & Simon, H. A. (1972). *Human Problem Solving.* Englewood Cliffs, NJ: Prentice-Hall.

Nicolaides, V. C., LaPort, K. A., Chen, T. R., Tomassetti, A. J., Weis, E. J., Zaccaro, S. J., & Cortina, J. M. (2014). The shared leadership of teams: A meta-analysis of proximal, distal, and moderating relationships. *The Leadership Quarterly, 25*(5), 923–942.

Pearce, C. L., & Conger, J. A. (2003). *Shared leadership: Reframing the hows and whys of leadership.* Thousand Oaks, CA: Sage.

Pink, D. H. (2009). *Drive: The surprising truth about what motivates us.* New York: Riverhead Books.

Reardon, S. F., Robinson-Cimpian, J. P., & Weathers, E. S. (2014). *Patterns and trends in racial/ethnic and socioeconomic academic achievement gaps.* Retrieved from https://cepa.stanford.edu/sites/default/files/reardon%20robinson-cimpian%20weathers%20HREFP%20chapter%20april2014.pdfhttps://cepa.stanford.edu/sites/default/files/reardon%20robinson-cimpian%20weathers%20HREFP%20chapter%20april2014.pdf

Reio, T. G., & Wiswell, A. (2000). Field investigation of the relationship among adult curiosity, workplace learning, and job performance. *Human Resource Development Quarterly, 11*(1) 5–30.

Rogers, E. M. (2003). *Diffusion of innovations* (5th ed.). New York: Free Press.

Seligman, M. (1990). *Learned optimism: How to change your mind and your life.* New York: Vintage Books.

Sinek, S. (2011). *Start with why: How great leaders inspire everyone to take action.* New York: Portfolio/Penguin.

Somech, A. (2006). The effects of leadership style and team process on performance and innovation in functionally heterogeneous teams. *Journal of Management, 32*(1), 132–157.

Spillane, J. P. (2000). *District leaders' perceptions of teacher learning* (CPRE Occasional Paper Series OP-05). Philadelphia: Consortium for Policy Research in Education.

Yosso, T. J. (2005). Whose culture has capital? A critical race theory discussion of community cultural wealth. *Race, Ethnicity and Education, 8*(1), 69–91.

Zhang, Z., Waldman, D. A., & Wang, Z. (2012). A multilevel investigation of leader–member exchange, informal leader emergence, and individual and team performance. *Personnel Psychology, 65*(1), 49–78.

About the Authors

Bryan Goodwin, CEO of McREL International, thrives on translating education research into practice, scanning the world for new insights and best practices, and helping educators everywhere adapt them to address their own challenges. A frequent conference presenter, he is the author of *Simply Better: Doing What Matters Most to Change the Odds for Student Success*, and co-author of *The 12 Touchstones of Good Teaching* and *Balanced Leadership for Powerful Learning: Tools for Achieving Success in Your School*. Before joining McREL in 1998, Bryan was a college instructor, a high school teacher, and a business journalist.

Kristin Rouleau is senior director of learning services and innovation at McREL International, working with schools, districts, and state departments of education as they navigate change and implement practices to increase student achievement. Kristin earned her administrative credentials from the University of Washington, her master's in curriculum and teaching from Michigan State University, and a bachelor's degree in elementary education from Western Michigan University. As of this writing, she is a doctoral student in leadership for educational equity at the University of Colorado–Denver.

Dale Lewis is senior director of research, evaluation, and technical assistance at McREL International, and is the deputy director of the Regional Educational Laboratory for the Pacific Region. Before joining McREL, Dale was a certified educational diagnostician, a special education teacher, a principal consultant for the American Institutes for Research, and director of the Texas Comprehensive Center. Dale has extensive experience using the Concerns-Based Adoption Model to support implementation of new education programs and initiatives.